Earth
To Eternity:

The Problems with Atheism and Evolution,
Compelling Evidence Christianity is True,
How the World Will Really End,
Plus, Answers to Tough Questions.

Dan Cote

EARTH TO ETERNITY
Copyright © 2010 by Daniel R. Cote

For additional copies and bulk purchases, contact the author at: dc.earthtoeternity@gmail.com

ISBN 978-1-60458-728-9

Printed in the United States of America by Instantpublisher.com

Acknowledgments

I would like to thank Jeff Liskin, Gill Bechard, Rich Gabelmann, Paul Parent, and Alexandra Cote for editorial comments and insights. I would especially like to thank Colleen Gundlach for her careful editing of the manuscript and Doug Aldrich for excellent theological and formatting suggestions.

To Nancy, Alexandra, and Erik with love.

CONTENTS

Introduction

Failed Approaches To The Origin Of Life

Evidence That the Bible Is From God

Evidence That Jesus Is God's Son

What Christianity Is All About

Sifting Through World Religions For Truth

More Motivation For Following Jesus

Introduction

Religion is a much debated topic in our time. Perhaps it has always been. Is it really possible that Jesus is the only way to God as Christianity claims? I certainly didn't believe it, but after years of study and research, I was swayed by the evidence. In the upcoming chapters I will lay out the case that, beyond the shadow of a doubt, Jesus is the only way to eternal life in the presence of God.

As individuals, we can probably all think of pivotal moments in the formation of our religious views. We probably all made life altering decisions about religion without the benefit of having all of the information. As a teenager, I became skeptical of what I had been taught as a child about God and religion. I certainly questioned if there was really a God. What I learned in school and from the media about evolution challenged my religious understanding of the origin of humanity. My skepticism about Jesus being the only way to God and the biblical creation stories reached a pinnacle in my twenties.

My journey back to Christianity began as a desire to learn the truth if it could be known. Perhaps I was partially motivated by fear that what I had been taught about Jesus and heaven and hell might be true. At any rate, I thought I could prove that all religions were really alike at their core—maybe I would even write a book about my findings—so I started researching different religions. My training in engineering and science necessitated that I have facts, evidence, and data. One day, on my way home from work in my car, I heard a Christian apologist (one who engages in the rational defense of Christianity) saying things on the radio that I had never heard or considered before. That is how it began for me. Needless to say, things didn't turn out the way I thought they would at the beginning of my search.

Introduction

As I delved into Christianity, I was amazed by the depth and breadth of the evidence supporting its unique truth. I could not be content with a cursory study of this issue so I undertook to earn a graduate degree in Christian apologetics.

My hope is to share what I have learned with anyone who is interested in what Christianity teaches, and the logic and evidence underpinning it. This book should also be useful for Christians who would like to share their faith with others.

My goal in writing this book has not been to write an exhaustive book, but instead, a simple one that presents important evidence and facts in a straightforward way. There are many great books about Christianity, but often they are written at a level that assumes prior knowledge of the subject, or their presentation is so detailed that they are difficult to follow unless you are immersed in the field.

I hope you will find that important topics ranging from atheism and evolution, to the resurrection and the end times, have been distilled down to a point where the essential issues and facts become clear, and that this clarity will help you better understand these issues and make important judgments about them.

It has been my experience that sometimes Christians are not direct enough in presenting Christianity. Consequently, the message is watered down, and as a result, never fully communicated. This is quite contrary to what the first followers of Jesus did. I will try to avoid that. Forgive me for being blunt at times.

You have nothing to lose by reading this small book. In a few hours of your time you can learn what Christianity is really about and gain an understanding of the evidence supporting it.

I hope that the truth is obvious by the time you finish this book. I invite you to email your questions and comments to me at dc.earthtoeternity@gmail.com. I will do my best to answer you.

Dan Cote

One
The Absurdity of Atheism and Agnosticism

In case you missed it in the introduction, my objective in this book is to prove beyond the shadow of a doubt that Christianity is true and that Jesus is the only way to eternal life in the presence of God.

Why Does It Matter if Christianity is True?

According to Jesus, all humans will spend eternity in the presence of God in a place of great joy, or separated from God in a very unpleasant place. According to Jesus, the decisions you make in this life will affect your eternal destiny. That is why it matters.

Before I lay out the case for Christianity, I need to focus on two things which obscure the truth: atheism and the Theory of Evolution. If atheism is true, then there is no God, and Christianity could not possibly be true. If the Theory of Evolution is true, the veracity of the Bible is called into question. In this chapter and the next, I will show that atheism is a false worldview and that the Theory of Evolution is a false theory. Then I will move on to powerful evidence that shows that Christianity and its claims are true.

An Expanding Universe Points to a Beginning

Up until the twentieth century, scientists widely accepted the steady-state model of the universe. The steady-state model supposed that the universe was infinitely old and unchanging—it just existed eternally. If it were infinitely old, then time and space would have no beginning. The universe would have always been and would always be. Since the universe was thought to be static and unchanging, stellar bodies such as stars

8

and galaxies would be maintained at fixed distances from each other. If time and space had no beginning, there would be no need of a creator.

The plausibility of the steady-state model of the universe was called into question as a result of the theoretical work of Albert Einstein and Georges Lemaitre which indicated that the universe must be expanding. Within decades, the predictions of Einstein and Lemaitre would be affirmed by experimental observations.

In 1929, Edwin Hubble observed by telescope that the universe was in fact expanding. He noted that galaxies were moving apart from each other. In 1964, Arno Penzias and Robert Wilson discovered the presence of cosmic microwave radiation indicative of the fact that the universe was once very hot. These scientific results along with others led scientists to posit that the universe had a near infinitely hot and compact beginning—our enormous universe started out in the distant past as small and hot. This explanation for the origin of the universe became known as the Big Bang Theory. It affirms that time and space had a beginning approximately 13.7 billion years ago, and that the universe continues to expand just like an explosion would.[1]

Is the Big Bang Theory ultimately correct about the beginning of the universe? Theories are refined as new data is collected, but it is certainly significant that cosmologists now almost universally agree that the universe had a beginning. For thousands of years, long before telescopes and space probes, the book of Genesis has affirmed this very thing: "In the beginning God created the heavens and the earth." (Genesis 1:1)

Principle of Causality

The Principle of Causality simply states that every effect has a cause.[2] It is an undeniable truth that nothing happens without a cause. Will your car ever start unless someone or something performs some action that causes it to start? Of course it will not. If you turn the key in the ignition, press the button on your remote starter, or perhaps just the right ignition wires short out, the car will start. In any case there is a cause for the effect (the starting of the car).

If the Principle of Causality were not true, science could not advance and problems could not be solved because you could never be sure that you had found the cause of an illness, or the cause of a train wreck. Illnesses and train wrecks could just be random effects, but in our modern scientific world, we know that events, illnesses, and train wrecks have a cause. You will be hard pressed to find anyone who denies the Principle of Causality.

A Big Problem for Atheists and Agnostics

An atheist denies the existence of God. An agnostic usually argues that whether God exists or not is unknown, or, denies that he or she can have knowledge of God.

The scientific conclusion that the universe had a beginning, coupled with the Principle of Causality presents a major problem for atheists and agnostics. Consider the following simple logical argument:

Premise 1:   Everything that begins to exist has a cause.
Premise 2:   The universe began to exist.
Conclusion: Therefore, the universe must have a cause.

If the two premises in this argument are true, and the construction of the argument is valid, then the conclusion must follow necessarily. Think about it for a moment. Is there any way out of the conclusion to this argument? The conclusion is undeniable. If the universe began to exist, something had to have caused it to exist.

What Could Have Caused the Universe?

One estimate of the number of stars in the universe is ten billion trillion, and some of these stars have diameters more than 200,000 times that of the earth. As a comparison, if the earth were the diameter of a golf ball, the largest known star would have a diameter equal to 24 times the height of the Empire State Building! The cause of the universe (the *Creator*) must be very great and powerful indeed!

So where does this leave atheists and agnostics? They are in the uncomfortable, irrational position of having to deny the Principle of Causality and the obvious conclusion that derives from it. It makes sense to say that *something* created the

10

universe. It makes no sense to say that *nothing* created the universe! That someone or something created the universe is undeniable—it began to exist.

Who Created the Creator?

The Creator of the universe must have existed before its creation, otherwise He could not have created it. There were no such things as time and space before the initiation of the universe since time and space are part and parcel of the universe. According to the Principle of Causality, only things that have a beginning need a cause. Beginning implies initiation in space and time. The Creator is outside of space and time because He existed prior to the initiation of space and time. Therefore, it makes no sense to talk about the beginning of such a being. The Creator must logically be a timeless being which means He must be an eternal being.

Another Problem for Atheists and Agnostics

Information is stored in many ways. If you visit a web page and derive information from it, that is only possible because the creator of the web page took the time to organize letters into sentences or to provide diagrams and pictures. In the ancient world, information was stored on stone or clay tablets using early forms of writing such as hieroglyphics or cuneiform. A program stored in a computer's memory contains digital codes that represent certain mathematical or logical operations. The computer programmer provides the information that tells the microprocessor what to do.

Information Comes From Intelligent Beings

In all of these instances (the web page, ancient tablet, or computer program), the source of the information is an intelligent being. In fact, when we trace back to the source of information, wherever it is contained, we always find that it was produced by an intelligent being. The reality is, there is no known source for information other than intelligent beings.[3] Who else creates magazines, web pages, or computer programs? Only intelligent beings—right?

Consider the human genome which is the complete DNA

sequence of an organism and contains its complete specification and heredity information. According to the Human Genome Project web page:

> The human genome is made up of DNA, which has four different chemical building blocks. These are called bases and abbreviated A, T, C, and G. In the human genome, about 3 billion bases are arranged along the chromosomes in a particular order for each unique individual. To get an idea of the size of the human genome present in each of our cells, consider the following analogy: If the DNA sequence of the human genome were compiled in books, the equivalent of 200 volumes the size of a Manhattan telephone book (at 1000 pages each) would be needed to hold it all. It would take about 9.5 years to read out loud (without stopping) the 3 billion bases in a person's genome sequence. This is calculated on a reading rate of 10 bases per second, equaling 600 bases/minute, 36,000 bases/hour, 864,000 bases/day, 315,360,000 bases/year.[4]

The genetic information content *present in each human cell* is the equivalent of 200 volumes, each the size of a Manhattan telephone book! It would take 9.5 years to read the sequence aloud! What a staggering amount of information is contained in every living organism. It should be obvious that there must be an intelligent source for the massive amount of information contained in the human genetic code. The logical argument looks like this:

Premise 1:   The only source of information is an intelligent being.

Premise 2:   The human genome contains a vast amount of information.

Conclusion: Therefore, the source of the human genome is an intelligent being.

Once again, if the two premises in this argument are true, and the construction of the argument is valid, then the conclusion must follow necessarily. Think about it for a moment. Is there any way out of the conclusion to this argument? The conclusion is undeniable. Here again, atheists and agnostics are left in the uncomfortable, irrational position of having to deny the obvious conclusion that humans were created by an intelligent being. The author of the human genome must be a vastly intelligent being. Christians call that being God.

Typically, when confronted with these kinds of logical arguments, atheists are quick to change the subject, but changing the subject will not invalidate the logical arguments above.

Some of the most important decisions individuals can make in their lives revolve around their views of God. Charting a course in life, starting with atheism or agnosticism as a presupposition, will subsequently lead to many incorrect decisions since they are clearly false.

Two
Evolution: A False Theory

If evolution is truly how humans came to be, then the Bible's story about the origin of humanity must be false, because evolution and Genesis contradict each other on many levels.

Christianity and Evolution Have Irreconcilable Differences

Genesis says that an all powerful God created humanity in His image. Genesis says that human beings are more than their bodies; they have an eternal component called the soul. Genesis says that God created complex creatures and plants fully formed according to their intended environment. Supporters of the Theory of Evolution would most likely deny all of these things.

Some have tried to reconcile the Bible's view of God with the Theory of Evolution, but in reality, Genesis and the Theory of Evolution have irreconcilable differences, and at every turn they contradict each other. This, of course means, that either Genesis or the Theory of Evolution is false. It is also logically possible that both Genesis and the Theory of Evolution are false. They must each be considered on their own merits. The validity of the Theory of Evolution will be considered in this chapter and the validity of the Bible which contains Genesis will be considered in Chapters 3 through 5.

Origin of Life According to Evolutionists

Let's start by summarizing what supporters of the Theory of Evolution typically say about the origin of humanity. Long ago, atoms combined into molecules, and those molecules combined to form more complex molecules. Then one day, billions of years ago, these molecules organized and came to life in the form of the first living organisms. About three billion years ago, through the fortunate bonding of molecules and atoms, simple cells were formed. Then more complex cells formed. Through random mutations and over billions of years, these simple living forms transformed by a long series of gradual changes into all of the organisms and plants that have ever lived.

According to evolutionary theory, all of this happened through natural selection acting on random mutations, gradually and over billions of years. Since all life is just the result of the proper combination of atoms and the random accidents of mutation, there is nothing beyond life. Humans are no more than the matter that makes them up, so when they die, that is it the end of their existence. Humans have no soul or spirit, so there is no afterlife. Human life just ends. Corpses decompose into simple compounds and elements once again, and the process of evolution marches on.

Evolution Eliminates God?

If all life evolved through natural selection operating on random mutations, there is no need for God. We are so used to hearing about evolution that many people just accept it as a fact. Some scientists even refer to the Theory of Evolution as the "fact of evolution," even though in science, theories can never be proven. Stephen Hawking, the famous physicist, explains that even a single repeatable observation can destroy the most grandiose theory.[5] Is the Theory of Evolution really a fact?

Could Evolution Produce the Human Genome?

Perhaps one of the best arguments to challenge the validity of the Theory of Evolution has already been presented. The human genome contains vast amounts of information which can only be the product of intelligence as was shown in Chapter 1. If the claims of evolutionists were true, the human genome would have to be the result of random mutations.

Consider the following simple random chance experiment. Let's say you put all of the three billion protein bases for the human genome, represented by the letters A, T, C and G, into a giant bag. What are the chances of pulling out of the bag, the base letters in the correct sequence for the complete 3 billion base sequence of the human genome, one base at a time? You could try as many times as you like but the probability of doing it just once in the entire age of the universe is virtually zero.

As an affirmation of the difficulty of explaining the formation of complex life structures like DNA through random processes, "…most origin-of-life researchers have decided to consider other theories that do not rely heavily on chance."[6]

You Need a Complete Cell Before It Can Evolve

Even if evolution really happened, you would need a complete, functioning, and living organism before it could take place. *Evolution supposedly works through natural selection operating on random mutations. Unless you have a living organism to begin with, there is nothing to mutate. So clearly, evolution could not be the explanation for the origin of the very first single cell organism.*

Author and philosopher, Stephen Meyer, estimates that the probability of forming a simple protein molecule through the random assembly of atoms to be one chance in 10^{125}, or one chance in *one* with 125 zeros after it. Meyer notes that 300 to 500 protein molecules would be required to build a simple cell. Moreover, only about 100 million years elapsed between the cooling of the Earth and the appearance of the first simple celled organisms.[7] The odds of the chance assemblage of a simple cell in a mere 100 million years are so poor that it would be truly miraculous if it happened by random means—but evolution does not allow miracles. Cleary a Creator is indicated in the formation of the first living cell. Supporters of evolution have not provided credible alternatives supported by evidence.

Grasping at Straws

In recognition of these problems some scientists suggest that the first cells came to the earth riding on meteorites. Suppose they did (not that there is any evidence that they did). That only moves the question of how life began from the earth to somewhere else in the universe where random chance will not have any better prospects of producing a living cell. A creative force in the initiation of life is obvious.

The Elephant in the Room: The Fossils Don't Fit

The fossils that have been dug from the ground over the last several hundred years tell us about the development and appearance of species in the distant past. These fossil discoveries are referred to as the "fossil record." The fossil record does not support the Theory of Evolution as will be shown through the words of some of the most influential advocates of evolution.

According to the Theory of Evolution, we should expect to find fossilized remains of "in between" species as, say for instance, sea creatures transform into land animals. Even today, we should see nature in confusion as existing species transition into new types of species. Instead of this continual transition and confusion of species, what we find are well defined species in the fossil record that appear fully formed with no evidence of evolution from a previous ancestor. Throughout time, species either go extinct, or remain to this day just as they originally appeared. This is obvious from the writings of Charles Darwin who raised this concern about his own theory, and in the writings of modern proponents of evolution such as Stephen Jay Gould and Richard Dawkins, as will be shown below.

The Cambrian Explosion: An Insurmountable Problem for Evolution

As noted above, the Theory of Evolution presupposes that creatures, starting from a single cell, evolved and transitioned into new species through many small modifications over a long period of time. What if a multitude of species showed up in the fossil record in a short time period with no signs of evolution from previous ancestors? Wouldn't that mean that evolution could not be the explanation for their appearance? That is exactly the problem faced by evolutionists in explaining a period in the history of the earth called the "Cambrian Explosion."

The Cambrian Explosion occurred about 530 million years ago. It is a geologically short time period where a vast number of complex, multi-celled organisms appeared on the earth. Its duration was a geological instant lasting five to ten million years. In this short period, most of the animal phyla (animal groups) that exist today appeared upon the earth. Creatures that rapidly appeared during the Cambrian Explosion include insects, shellfish, starfish, worms, and vertebrates.[8]

The Cambrian Explosion presents a serious problem for the Theory of Evolution. Complex creatures appeared without adequate time to evolve. Whole phyla and classes appeared with no predecessors. The creatures that existed before the Cambrian Explosion were simple single and multi-celled organisms with no ancestral link to the creatures that appeared during the Cambrian Explosion. In a nutshell, the transitional fossils (fossils of species undergoing change resulting in new species) that would be expected if the creatures of the Cambrian Explosion arrived on the scene via evolution are non-existent.[9]

Some scientists have argued that the creatures existing just before the Cambrian Explosion did not fossilize because they had soft bodies. This argument fails since small, soft-bodied creatures of earlier geological eras are represented in the fossil record.[10]

The Theory of Evolution as envisioned by Darwin fails to explain the rapid appearance of creatures in the Cambrian period. So why does Darwin's unsupported theory retain such a strong grip on modern science? Read on for the answer.

Darwin Admits the Fossil Record Doesn't Support His Theory

Darwin knew that the fossil record did not support his theory even in the 1860's. In *Origin of the Species,* Darwin voices his concern at the lack of transitional forms in the fossil record. He says:

> ...why, if species have descended from other species by insensibly fine gradations, do we not everywhere see innumerable transitional forms? Why is not all nature in confusion instead of the species being, as we see them, well defined?[11]

From his own words, it is obvious Darwin understood that evidence for his theory was seriously lacking. Darwin, writing just after the American Civil War, assumed that future discoveries of fossils would affirm his theory. But has that been the case? Clearly not, as eminent scientists Gould and Dawkins affirm below.

18

Evolution: A False Theory
Gould Reiterates the Fossil Problem in the 1980's
Fast forward more than 100 years to the 1980's. By then, surely, paleontologists would have found supporting evidence for Darwin's Theory of Evolution. However, we find leading paleontologist and Harvard professor Stephen Jay Gould describing the same lack of transitional forms in the fossil record. In *The Panda's Thumb*, Gould writes:

> The extreme rarity of transitional forms in the fossil record persists as the trade secret of paleontology. The evolutionary trees that adorn our textbooks have data only at the tips of the nodes of their branches; the rest is inference, however reasonable, not the evidence of fossils. Yet Darwin was so wedded to gradualism that he wagered his entire theory on a denial of this literal record...[12]

Gould affirms that the gradual transition between species postulated by Darwin is not found in the fossil record. He refers to this fact as "the trade secret of paleontology." According to Gould, Darwin denied the clear evidence from the fossil record which showed that creatures did not evolve through small gradual steps.

According to Gould,

> The history of most fossil species includes two features particularly inconsistent with gradualism:
> 1. Stasis. Most species exhibit no directional change during their tenure on earth. They appear in the fossil record looking much the same as when they disappear; morphological change is usually limited and directionless.
> 2. Sudden appearance. In any local area, a species does not arise gradually by steady transformation of its ancestors; it appears all at once and 'fully formed.'[13]

From Gould's own words, we learn that transitional forms are extremely rare, gradualism is not found in the fossil record, and creatures appear on the scene fully formed without having undergone evolutionary descent from earlier creatures.

Gould continued his belief in evolution, but he abandoned Darwin's gradualism because the fossil record does not support it. Gould was led by the lack of transitional fossil evidence to advance "punctuated equilibrium" as the means to explain the

Earth To Eternity

abrupt appearance of new species.

According to the theory of punctuated equilibrium, species remain the same for long periods of time, but sometimes undergo periods of rapid change. It was Gould's attempt to explain away problems in the fossil record and the lack of transitional forms.

In short, punctuated equilibrium is merely the naturalist's way of explaining the sudden appearance of fully formed species throughout the history of the earth without admitting the possibility of a Creator.

Dawkins Affirms the Fossil Problem and Admits Evolution is Really a Means of Denying God

That atheism is at the root of what sustains and perpetuates the Theory of Evolution is made abundantly clear in the words of leading evolutionist and Oxford professor, Richard Dawkins. Speaking about the gaps in the fossil record (the lack of transitional forms between species), Dawkins rails against Gould's punctuated equilibrium, but he affirms that the gaps are real. Consider the words of Richard Dawkins from his book, *The Blind Watchmaker*:

> My point here is that, when we are talking about gaps of this magnitude, there is no difference whatever in the interpretations of 'punctuationists' and 'gradualist'. Both schools of thought despise so-called scientific creationists equally, and both agree that the major gaps are real, that they are true imperfections in the fossil record. Both schools of thought agree that the only alternative explanation of the sudden appearance of so many complex animal types in the Cambrian era is divine creation, and both would reject this alternative.[14]

Dawkins affirms that the gaps in the fossil record are inconsistent with evolution, and, as Dawkins rightly observes above, the only alternative to evolution is divine creation. If you are an atheistic or agnostic scientist, you certainly cannot go there. That is what evolution is really all about for some scientists—a plausible means of denying the necessity of a Creator. They will invoke and advance anything to avoid God, so the evolutionist places his faith in a theory clearly contradicted by the fossil data.

Evolution: A False Theory

The evolutionist believes that which he has not seen, cannot reproduce, and cannot support with fossil data. His belief in evolution is based in faith, and thus, the religion of some scientists is evolution.

The Logic Regarding Evolution is Obvious

From the words of the evolutionists themselves, evolution is a theory with serious problems. Let's put what has been said into a simple logical argument:

Premise 1:   If the Theory of Evolution is correct, the fossil record should contain nearly countless transitional forms.

Premise 2:   Evolutionists affirm the "extreme rarity" of transitional forms in the fossil record.

Conclusion: Therefore, the validity of the Theory of Evolution is highly questionable.

The only reason we do not categorically state that the Theory of Evolution is false at this point is because it is possible that the countless missing transitional forms could appear in new fossil finds. However, the harsh reality is that it has been 150 years since Darwin formulated his theory, and Gould and Dawkins complain about the same gaps in the fossil record and the same lack of transitional forms. The picture is bleak. Any other scientific theory that failed to explain scientific findings for a century and a half would have died a natural death, but evolution continues to be promoted by much of the scientific establishment. Why? Because many scientists reject the possibility of divine creation, the only other alternative to evolution as Dawkins observes. We see here the reality that the scientific establishment is not so open-minded after all in its search for truth.

Many Credible Scientists Doubt the Validity of Evolution

The walls of the fortress around the Theory of Evolution are gradually being dismantled. Many competent scientists see it as a theory in crisis because of the reasons described above among others. Since 2001, hundreds of credible scientists from respected institutions all over the world have signed their names to the following statement:

A Scientific Dissent From Darwinism

We are skeptical of claims for the ability of random mutation and natural selection to account for the complexity of life. Careful examination of the evidence for Darwinian theory should be encouraged.

You can read about *A Scientific Dissent From Darwinism* and view the names and positions of the dissenting scientists at: www.dissentfromdarwin.org

Like atheism, charting a course in life starting with evolution as a presupposition, will lead to many incorrect decisions since it is clearly a false theory.

Three
The Bible: A Divine Book—Prophecies Speak Volumes

Are all of the religious books written over the last several thousand years equal? Is the Bible really no different than the *Quran*, the *Book of Mormon*, or the Hindu Veda? Isn't the Bible just another religious book among many religious books of questionable origin? I believe the answer to all of these questions can be shown to be a resounding "No."

How Could We Know That a Book is from God?

As the title to this chapter implies, I believe that the Bible can be shown to be a message from God. One of the most compelling proofs for the divine origin of the Bible is that it contains hundreds of prophecies that have shown to be accurate as will be shown below with specific examples.

A prophecy is a prediction about the future. There are about 1,000 prophecies in the Bible. They are about the Messiah (the Servant of the Lord who Christians recognize as Jesus Christ—more on that later), about nations and peoples, and about world events, past, present, and future. A large portion of these prophecies have been fulfilled in the last several thousand years. The rest are appointed for the future. That the Bible contains predictive prophecy makes it unique, as theologians Norman Geisler and William Nix indicate:

> Other books claim divine inspiration, such as the Koran, the Book of Mormon, and parts of the Veda. But none of those books contains predictive prophecy. As a result, fulfilled prophecy is a strong indication of the unique, divine authority of the Bible.[15]

I believe God is sending a message to you and me. He has made a way for us to know that the Bible is the true record of

23

Earth To Eternity

His revelation to humanity. The God of the Bible is a God of reason. He calls people to use their minds to seek Him and find Him.

In my own personal journey, I have found the clear record of fulfilled prophecy to be a very compelling piece of evidence showing the Bible to be from God. Who else could foretell the future and be right 100% of the time? Nostradamus's prophecies are vague and confusing and subject to being twisted to say whatever the interpreter is trying to prove. In contrast, many biblical prophecies are straightforward as I think you will see below.

Types of Prophecy

There are two broad groups of prophecies in the Bible: general prophecies and Messianic prophecies. General prophecies deal with Israel's fortunes and future, Jerusalem, the nations of the ancient world, and the events of the end times. Messianic prophecies deal with the coming Servant of the Lord who would suffer and die as payment for the sins of the world and later rule the earth.

Christians believe that Jesus Christ is a unique individual in history and that He is the subject of the Messianic prophecies. The word Messiah is from the Hebrew word that means "anointed one." While there are other people the Bible speaks of as anointed, there is a special individual, a great Messiah, who is to be a savior of His people. The Bible is very clear that the Messiah is to be a savior not only for the Jews but also for the Gentiles.[16] The English word Christ derives from the Greek word *Christos,* which means Messiah. Jesus is called Christ because Christians believe that He is the Messiah of the Old Testament who was anointed by God to bring salvation to the world.[17] Jesus fulfills both missions of the Messiah. At His first coming, Jesus came as a suffering servant who died to pay for the sins of humanity. At His second coming, Jesus will return as a conquering king and mighty ruler who will establish His kingdom on earth and bring about peace.

Who Were the Prophets?

The prophets came from all walks of life and had a wide

24

range of personalities and occupations. What they had in common was that they were God's spokesmen to the people. They were called directly by God. God revealed His message for the people to the prophets, and used their unique personalities and skills to communicate this message to the people. The message was often given for the purpose of correcting behavior that was unpleasing to God. The prophets received revelation from God through visions, dreams, and direct communication.

The authenticity and authority of a prophet was confirmed by the accuracy of his prophecies. An individual who gave false predictions was considered a false prophet. False prophets were not taken lightly in Bible times. The penalty for uttering false prophecies was death.[18] God did not want individuals to falsely claim that they were speaking for Him for personal gain and thus mislead the people.

When Were the Prophecies Written?

The prophecies contained in the Bible were written during the lives of the authors. A large fraction of biblical prophecy is found in the Old Testament writings of Moses, David, and the prophets. Moses wrote the Pentateuch (the first five books of the Bible) before 1400 B.C. The Psalms of David, which contain many prophecies, were written about 1000 B.C. The writing prophets (Isaiah, Jeremiah, Ezekiel, Daniel, Hosea, Joel, Amos, Obadiah, Jonah, Micah, Nahum, Habakkuk, Zephaniah, Haggai, Zechariah, and Malachi) lived and wrote their books during the period between the ninth and fifth century before Christ.

You will run across liberal Bible critics who will claim significantly later dates for the writing of these books. They typically assign later dates to these books because they reject the obvious supernatural implications of books that predict the future, not because the evidence leads them in that direction. The arguments that liberal scholars give in support of these later dates have been refuted by conservative Bible scholars.

Even if one were to accept later dates for the writing of the Old Testament books, the Dead Sea Scrolls clearly show (see Chapter 4) that they existed long before the birth of Christ. Therefore, we have in the Dead Sea Scrolls, indisputable

Earth To Eternity

physical evidence that many prophecies were written long before the events they predicted.

As theologian Norman Geisler observes:

> Even the most liberal critics admit that the prophetic books were completed some 400 years before Christ, and the Book of Daniel by about 167 B.C. Though there is good evidence to date most of these books much earlier (some of the psalms and earlier prophets were in the eighth and ninth centuries B.C.), what difference would it make? It is just as hard to predict an event 200 years in the future as it is to predict one that is 800 years in the future. Both feats would require nothing less than divine knowledge.[19]

Ten Specific Examples of Fulfilled Prophecy in the Bible

In my view, any open-minded individual, after looking at the fulfilled prophecies described in this chapter and the next will have to conclude that the Bible is not merely a human book. If the Bible is not merely a human book, then it requires very close attention and scrutiny, because what is found in the Bible cannot be found in any other book on the face of the earth. Let's start by taking a look at ten specific prophecies and their fulfillment. For each prophecy, I have provided the approximate date the prophecy was written, the Bible text of the prophecy, an explanation of the prophecy, and a summary of how it was fulfilled.

Prophecy 1: The Re-gathering of Israel

Date of Prophecy: 592-570 B.C.

Bible Text: Ezekiel 36:22-24 (also Ezekiel 11:14-18)

...Thus says the Lord God, "It is not for your sake, O house of Israel, that I am about to act, but for My holy name, which you have profaned among the nations where you went....the nations will know that I am the Lord," declares the Lord God, "when I prove Myself holy among you in their sight. For I will take you from the nations, gather you from all the lands and bring you into your own land."

The Bible: A Divine Book—Prophecies Speak Volumes

Summary of Prophecy

Many amazing prophecies are made about the nation of Israel in the Old Testament, but perhaps one of the most amazing predicts the re-gathering of the people of Israel from the countries of the world. Writing in the sixth century before the birth of Christ, God says to Israel through the prophet Ezekiel that they would once again be brought into their own land of Palestine from the lands and nations where they had been scattered.

Fulfillment

In A.D. 70, the Roman general Titus crushed a Jewish revolt and destroyed the Temple in Jerusalem. Many Jews were killed and the Jews living in Israel were dispersed throughout the world. For nearly 1800 years, the Jews remained dispersed throughout the nations of the earth. They have been persecuted in many places and often suffered exile from the nations where they resettled. Six million Jews were killed in the holocaust alone.

In the 1800's, Jews from around the world began immigrating to Israel. In 1948, the United Nations voted to divide Palestine into a Jewish and Palestinian state. Against all odds, Israel once again became a nation and has been under attack ever since because many of her neighbors refuse to accept her right to exist.[20] A massive wave of Jewish immigration from many nations to Israel commenced in 1948 and has continued to this day.

Prophecy 2: Birth Place of the Messiah

Date of Prophecy: 700 B.C.

Bible Text: Micah 5:2-5:4

But as for you, Bethlehem Ephrathah, *too* little to be among the clans of Judah, from you One will go forth for Me to be ruler in Israel. His goings forth are from long ago, From the days of eternity.... And He will arise and shepherd His flock in the strength of the Lord, in the majesty of the name of the Lord His God.... He will be great to the ends of the earth.

Earth To Eternity

Summary of Prophecy

From the tiny, insignificant town of Bethlehem would come an eternal being (meaning that He existed before creation). Ephrathah is the ancient name of Bethlehem. We learn that this eternal being will be ruler in Israel. He will shepherd His flock with the power and majesty of God and His greatness will extend to the ends of the earth.

Fulfillment

Jesus Christ was born in Bethlehem. That part of the prophecy is fulfilled. Jesus came as God in the flesh and as the King of the Jews, a fact He affirmed in his trial before Pontius Pilate. Jesus proved that He was God by rising from the dead (see Chapter 7). Since Jesus is God, He is an eternal being, meaning He existed before the creation of the universe. While the Jews rejected Him at His first coming, the whole world will be under Jesus' dominion at His Second Coming.

Prophecy 3: Destruction of Jerusalem

Date of Prophecy: 700 B.C.

Text: Micah 3:9-12

Now hear this, heads of the house of Jacob and rulers of the house of Israel, who abhor justice and twist everything that is straight, who build Zion with bloodshed and Jerusalem with violent injustice. Her leaders pronounce judgment for a bribe, her priests instruct for a price and her prophets divine for money. Yet they lean on the LORD saying, "Is not the LORD in our midst? Calamity will not come upon us." Therefore, on account of you Zion will be plowed as a field, Jerusalem will become a heap of ruins, and the mountain of the temple *will become* high places of a forest.

Summary of Prophecy

The prophecy is addressed to the house Jacob and its rulers. In the Old Testament, when God blessed Jacob, He changed his name to Israel. The twelve patriarchs of the twelve tribes of Israel were sons of Jacob, so the prophecy is addressing the leaders of Israel.

In this prophecy, Zion and Jerusalem are synonymous. The prophet Micah, speaking for the Lord, condemns the injustice and evil ways of the priests, prophets, and leaders of Israel, and in particular those of Jerusalem, the capital of Israel. The rulers are complacent, thinking that they have the Lord on their side. Because of their evil, God will allow Jerusalem and the temple to be destroyed and overgrown.

Fulfillment

Nebuchadnezzar ruled the Babylonian Empire from 605-562 B.C. From the beginning of his rule, Nebuchadnezzar harassed, raided, and finally destroyed Jerusalem in 586 B.C. He deported and resettled a large number of Jews, using them as slaves for his various building projects. Jerusalem was looted and the bronze pillars of the temple along with the bronze, gold, and silver implements from the temple were broken up and carried to Babylon. All of the houses in Jerusalem and the temple were burned. Nebuchadnezzar's army broke down the walls of the city around Jerusalem.[21] Jerusalem lay in ruins and was desolate from the destruction of Jerusalem in 586 B.C., until the Jews were allowed by the Persian king Cyrus to return to rebuild the temple in 538 B.C. About 50,000 Jews returned to Jerusalem and arrived there in 536 B.C. to begin the rebuilding of the temple.

Prophecy 4: Continuance of the Jews

Date of Prophecy: 1450-1410 B.C.

Text: Leviticus 26:41-45

Speaking of the Jews, God says through Moses:

> … if their uncircumcised heart becomes humbled so that they then make amends for their iniquity, then I will remember My covenant with Jacob, and I will remember also My covenant with Isaac, and My covenant with Abraham as well, and I will remember the land…. They… meanwhile, will be making amends for their iniquity, because they rejected My ordinances and their soul abhorred My statutes. Yet in spite of this, when they are in the land of their enemies, I will not reject them, nor will I so

Earth To Eternity

abhor them as to destroy them, breaking My covenant with them; for I am the Lord their God. But I will remember for them the covenant with their ancestors, whom I brought out of the land of Egypt in the sight of the nations, that I might be their God. I am the Lord.

Summary of Prophecy

The Old Testament prophesied that the Jews would survive. God said that He would punish the Jews if they disobeyed Him and worshipped other gods, but He also promised to sustain and protect a remnant throughout the ages.

In the Book of Leviticus, God conveys to the Jews the conditions for remaining in fellowship with Him. God is holy and He required obedience and faithfulness from His chosen people with whom He had made a covenant. God promised to bless the Jews if they were faithful to Him and His laws, and He promised to punish them if they disobeyed. God's objective in punishment is clearly to bring His people to repentance so that they will humble themselves before Him. God promised to never completely destroy the Jews because He made a covenant with them—He promised there would always be a remnant of the Jews.

Fulfillment

The Jews trace their origin to Abraham over 4,000 years ago. During that time, empires have risen and fallen and political boundaries have been drawn and redrawn. The Jews were conquered and dispersed from their own land by ancient empires that have come and gone. They have been kicked out repeatedly from European nations where they sought asylum. They have been persecuted and murdered throughout history, and yet they survive to this day. No other group in the world has maintained its national and religious identity over a 4,000 year period. That the Jews survive to this day is truly miraculous, but completely to be expected according to this and other prophecies.

The survival of the Jews to this day, in particular, the rebirth of the Jewish nation in 1948 is truly amazing. Precisely what Moses prophesied about the Jews has been fulfilled completely!

The Bible: A Divine Book—Prophecies Speak Volumes
Prophecy 5: The Destruction of Tyre, an Important City North of Israel

Bible Text: Ezekiel 26:1-15

Now in the eleventh year, on the first of the month, the word of
the Lord came to me saying, "Son of man, because Tyre has said
concerning Jerusalem, 'Aha, the gateway of the peoples is broken;
it has opened to me. I shall be filled, now that she is laid waste,'
therefore thus says the Lord God, 'Behold, I am against you, O
Tyre, and I will bring up many nations against you, as the sea
brings up its waves. They will destroy the walls of Tyre and break
down her towers; and I will scrape her debris from her and make
her a bare rock. She will be a place for the spreading of nets in the
midst of the sea, for I have spoken,' declares the Lord God, 'and
she will become spoil for the nations. Also her daughters who are
on the mainland will be slain by the sword, and they will know
that I am the Lord.' " For thus says the Lord God, "Behold, I will
bring upon Tyre from the north Nebuchadnezzar king of Babylon,
king of kings, with horses, chariots, cavalry and a great army. He
will slay your daughters on the mainland with the sword; and he
will make siege walls against you, cast up a ramp against you and
raise up a large shield against you. The blow of his battering rams
he will direct against your walls, and with his axes he will break
down your towers. Because of the multitude of his horses, the dust
raised by them will cover you; your walls will shake at the noise
of cavalry and wagons and chariots when he enters your gates as
men enter a city that is breached. With the hoofs of his horses he
will trample all your streets. He will slay your people with the
sword; and your strong pillars will come down to the ground.
Also they will make a spoil of your riches and a prey of your
merchandise, break down your walls and destroy your pleasant
houses, and throw your stones and your timbers and your debris
into the water. So I will silence the sound of your songs, and the
sound of your harps will be heard no more. I will make you a bare
rock; you will be a place for the spreading of nets. You will be
built no more, for I the Lord have spoken," declares the Lord God.
Thus says the Lord God to Tyre, "Shall not the coastlands shake
at the sound of your fall when the wounded groan, when the
slaughter occurs in your midst?"

Date of Prophecy: About 586 B.C.

Earth To Eternity

Summary of Prophecy

The residents of Tyre took pleasure in the destruction of Israel. God would punish them for doing so. The prophet Ezekiel records God's decree that Tyre would be laid waste by the "nations" who would be brought against her. The island portion of Tyre was to be scraped to the bare rock and destined to become a place for the spreading of fish nets in the midst of the sea. The Lord declares that Nebuchadnezzar, the king of Babylon, would slay the inhabitants on the mainland and destroy the houses. Stone and timber would be thrown into the water and Tyre would never be rebuilt.

Fulfillment

For thirteen years spanning 585 B.C. through 572 B.C., Nebuchadnezzar, king of Babylon, besieged the mainland portion of Tyre and finally destroyed it. Later in 332 B.C., Alexander the Great besieged and destroyed the island portion of Tyre, 350 years after Ezekiel's prophecy. He gained access to it by building a causeway to the island of stone and wood materials scraped from the mainland into the sea. While areas around Tyre have been rebuilt, the city itself remains in ruins. Here again, the Bible's prophecy about Tyre was completely fulfilled [22]

Prophecy 6: Purging the Altar at Bethel of Idol Worship

Bible Text: 1 Kings 13:1-2

> Now behold, there came a man of God from Judah to Bethel by the word of the Lord, while Jeroboam was standing by the altar to burn incense. He cried against the altar by the word of the Lord, and said, "O altar, altar, thus says the Lord, 'Behold, a son shall be born to the house of David, Josiah by name; and on you he shall sacrifice the priests of the high places who burn incense on you, and human bones shall be burned on you.' "

Date of Prophecy: About 930 B.C.

Summary of Prophecy

A prophet of God prophesies 300 years in advance that a son of David (a descendent of David) named Josiah would purge

32

The Bible: A Divine Book—Prophecies Speak Volumes

the altar in Bethel of idol worship. He would sacrifice the priests of the high places on it, and burn their bones upon the altar.

Fulfillment

The fulfillment of this prophecy takes place in about 620 B.C. and is recorded in 2 Kings 23:16-20.[23] Exactly as prophesied hundreds of years earlier, Josiah, King of Judah and descendent of David, cleansed the temple at Bethel of idol worship. Exactly as prophesied, Josiah slaughtered the priests of the high places and burned their bones on the altar at Bethel.

This may seem to be a violent and gruesome act, but is justified in the light that the Jews were God's chosen people. God had made a covenant with them that if they remained faithful, they would retain His blessing. In the first of the Ten Commandments, God makes it clear to the Israelites that they must have no other gods. The idol worship at Bethel was a grave sin. The priests of the high places led the people and the nation of Israel astray. They were affecting the eternal destiny of the Israelites and thus needed to be destroyed to preserve the nation.

Prophecy 7: Jesus: A Savior for the World

Date of Prophecy: 740-680 B.C.

Bible Text: Isaiah 49:5-6

> And now says the Lord, who formed Me from the womb to be His Servant, to bring Jacob back to Him, so that Israel might be gathered to Him…He says, "It is too small a thing that You should be My Servant to raise up the tribes of Jacob and to restore the preserved ones of Israel; I will also make You a light of the nations so that My salvation may reach to the end of the earth."

Summary of Prophecy

As noted previously, the tribes of Jacob comprised the Nation of Israel. Speaking through the prophet Isaiah, the Servant of the Lord (the Messiah, i.e. Jesus) says that God has told Him that He has much greater plans for Him than merely bringing salvation to the Jews. The purpose of the Servant will be to extend salvation to the very ends of the earth, meaning all the nations of the world.

Earth To Eternity

Fulfillment

Before Jesus ascended into heaven, He gave His disciples this command,

All authority has been given to Me in heaven and on earth. Go therefore and make disciples of all the nations, baptizing them in the name of the Father and the Son and the Holy Spirit, teaching them to observe all that I commanded you; and lo, I am with you always, even to the end of the age. (Matthew 28:18-20)

Jesus' disciples quickly spread the light of the gospel, which is the good news that salvation is available to all those who repent of their sins and truly believe in the death and resurrection of Jesus. In many cases, the disciples risked their lives to speak what they believed to be the truth. Many died as martyrs because they refused to recant their testimony about Jesus (more on that in Chapter 7). Today, the words of the prophet Isaiah have been fulfilled for Christianity has been spread to virtually every nation on earth and its boundaries continue to expand. Approximately 33% of the world's population now claims Christian affiliation. In places where the church is oppressed, as in China and Africa, growth is rapid.

Prophecy 8: Prediction of the 70 Year Babylonian Exile of the Jews

Date of Prophecy: 605 B.C.

Bible Text: Jeremiah 25:8-11

Therefore thus says the LORD of hosts, "Because you have not obeyed My words, behold, I will send and take all the families of the north," declares the LORD, "and *I will send* to Nebuchadnezzar king of Babylon, My servant, and will bring them against this land and against its inhabitants and against all these nations round about; and I will utterly destroy them and make them a horror and a hissing, and an everlasting desolation. Moreover, I will take from them the voice of joy and the voice of gladness, the voice of the bridegroom and the voice of the bride, the sound of the millstones and the light of the lamp. This whole land will be a desolation and a horror, and these nations will serve the king of Babylon seventy years."

The Bible: A Divine Book—Prophecies Speak Volumes

Summary of Prophecy

The northern part of Israel had already been destroyed over one hundred years earlier by the Assyrians. What was left of Israel was the southern kingdom of Judah whose capital was Jerusalem. Through the prophet Jeremiah, God announces that Judah would be attacked and destroyed by Nebuchadnezzar, King of Babylon. The normal sounds of life and its joys would be silenced in a horrible way and the Jews would become slaves to the king of Babylon for 70 years.

Fulfillment

Beginning in 605 B.C., the Jews were held captive in Babylon for 70 years. The Jews were still there when Babylon was conquered by the Persians. In 538 B.C., Cyrus, the king of Persia, conquered Babylon and issued a decree allowing the Jews to return to their homeland to rebuild the temple. They arrived in Jerusalem in 536 B.C., 70 years after the beginning of their exile, and thus the prophecy was fulfilled exactly as given.

Prophecy 9: Naming the Persian King Who Would Release the Jews over 150 Years in Advance

Date of Prophecy: 740-680 B.C.

Bible Text: Isaiah 45:1-13

Thus says the LORD to Cyrus His anointed, whom I have taken by the right hand, to subdue nations before him and to loose the loins of kings; to open doors before him so that gates will not be shut: "I will go before you and make the rough places smooth" .... Thus says the LORD, the Holy One of Israel, and his Maker: "Ask Me about the things to come concerning My sons, and you shall commit to Me the work of My hands. It is I who made the earth, and created man upon it. I stretched out the heavens with My hands And I ordained all their host. I have aroused him [Cyrus] in righteousness and I will make all his ways smooth; He will build My city and will let My exiles go free, Without any payment or reward," says the LORD of hosts.

Summary of Prophecy

Speaking through the prophet Isaiah, God names Cyrus as

35

Earth To Eternity

the world ruler He would raise up to free His sons (the Jews) from their still future exile at the hands of Nebuchadnezzar, king of Babylon. When Isaiah wrote this prophecy in about 700 B.C., the Assyrians were still the dominant world power, the Babylonian empire was still to rise and fall, and the future great king of Persia, Cyrus, who would conquer Babylon and free the Jews, had not even been born.

Fulfillment

The Assyrians were eclipsed by Nebuchadnezzar and the Babylonians. In 539 B.C., the Babylonian Empire fell to Cyrus the Great, ruler of the Persian Empire. As noted above, in 538 B.C., Cyrus issued a decree allowing the Jews to return to their homeland to rebuild the temple exactly as was foretold by the prophet Isaiah. The "Cyrus Cylinder," an important archaeological artifact discovered in Babylon, records the edicts of Cyrus and describes the Persian policy of allowing displaced peoples to return to their native lands to rebuild temples and sanctuaries.[24] Thus the prophecy was fulfilled.

Prophecy 10: Dating the Messiah's Execution and the Destruction of Jerusalem—*Perhaps One of the Greatest Prophecies*

Date of Prophecy: 537 B.C.

Bible Text: Daniel 9:24-26

Seventy weeks have been decreed for your people and your holy city, to finish the transgression, to make an end of sin, to make atonement for iniquity, to bring in everlasting righteousness, to seal up vision and prophecy and to anoint the most holy place. So you are to know and discern that from the issuing of a decree to restore and rebuild Jerusalem until Messiah the Prince there will be seven weeks and sixty-two weeks; it will be built again, with plaza and moat, even in times of distress. Then after the sixty-two weeks the Messiah will be cut off and have nothing, and the people of the prince who is to come will destroy the city and the sanctuary. And its end will come with a flood; even to the end there will be war; desolations are determined.

Summary of Prophecy

Daniel 9:24-26 records the prophet's vision concerning his

36

The Bible: A Divine Book—Prophecies Speak Volumes
people and the Messiah. In the context of the prophecy, each "week" represents seven years. Daniel is visited by Gabriel who tells him that the Messiah will be cut off (killed), 69 weeks (7 weeks + 62 weeks = 69 weeks) from the issuing of a decree to restore and rebuild Jerusalem.

Fulfillment

Theologian Harold Hoehner demonstrates that this prophecy is fulfilled exactly.[25] The Jews originally used a lunar calendar. The 69 weeks, then, is equal to 483 lunar years (69 x 7 = 483). When this time period is converted to solar years (365 day per year as in our current calendar), a reduced span of 476 years is anticipated between the issuing of a decree to restore and rebuild Jerusalem, to the time when the Messiah would be cut off or killed.

Decrees were issued by Persian kings regarding the rebuilding of the temple and Jerusalem. As noted earlier, Cyrus issued such a decree allowing the Jews to return to rebuild the temple in Jerusalem. It was reaffirmed by Darius, a successor of Cyrus. It was the later Persian king Artaxerxes however, who specifically issued a decree allowing the rebuilding of the fortifications and the walls of the city of Jerusalem. This decree was issued to Nehemiah by Artaxerxes in 444 B.C. The Messiah was killed exactly 476 years later when Jesus Christ was crucified in A.D. 33. More than 500 years in advance, the Book of Daniel reveals the exact timing of the crucifixion of Jesus Christ![26]

A Perfect Track Record

The track record for the fulfillment of Bible prophecy is perfect. What I have presented above is a small sample of the many prophecies found in the Bible. All of the prophecies except the end time prophecies have been fulfilled (more on that in Chapter 14). Only an all-powerful, all-knowing Being could foretell the future way in advance and then cause events to work out exactly as prophesied. The Bible is certainly God's book.

Read on for more examples of fulfilled prophecies.

Four
The Bible: A Divine Book—Messianic Prophecy

Specific Prophecies about the Messiah

As discussed in the previous chapter, Messianic prophecies deal with the coming Servant of the Lord who would suffer but also rule the earth. Christians believe that Jesus Christ is the unique individual in the history of the world that is the subject of the Messianic prophecies. The reason will be obvious below.

From the beginning to the end of the Old Testament, a major theme of the Bible is the Savior that would come to reconcile man to God. The Messiah is that Savior, and the events of the life of Jesus Christ clearly testify that He was the Savior of the world promised by God through the prophets.

The Bible contains over 100 prophecies about the coming Messiah that God would send into the world. The table below shows ten of these. The probability that 48 of the Messianic prophecies would be randomly fulfilled in the life of a single individual is 1 in 10^{157} (More on this in Chapter 6).

Given the huge improbability of an individual fulfilling all of the Messianic prophecies, we should expect that not even a single individual in the entire history of the world could have fulfilled them all. Yet Jesus Christ fulfilled all of these prophecies with the exception of those about His Second Coming which are appointed for the future. This clearly identifies Him as the Messiah predicted by the prophets and sent by God.[27]

The table below provides a sample of this astonishing set of prophecies written hundreds of years before Jesus was born. This is unmatched by any other religious book. The table lists the prophecy, its location in the Old Testament, and the location in the New Testament passage describing its fulfillment.

38

Sample of Ten Messianic Prophecies

Prophecy Concerning Messiah	Old Testament Prophecy	New Testament Fulfillment
Messiah will be born to a virgin	Isaiah 7:14	Matthew 1:23
Messiah will be born in Bethlehem	Micah 5:2	Matthew 2:1,6
Messiah will enter Jerusalem to a rejoicing crowd and riding on a colt	Zechariah 9:9	Matthew 21:1-11
Messiah will be betrayed for 30 pieces of silver	Zechariah 11:12-13	Matthew 26:14-16
Messiah to be offered drink mixed with gall	Psalm 69:21	Matthew 27:34
Messiah's clothes to be gambled for	Psalm 22:18	Matthew 27:35
Messiah's trust in God to be mocked	Psalm 22:7-8	Matthew 27:43
Messiah's hands and feet to be pierced	Psalm 22:16	John 19:34
Messiah's grave to be among the rich	Isaiah 53:9	Matthew 27:57-60
Messiah will be resurrected	Psalm 16:10	Acts 2:24-28

A Book that Predicts the Future is a Supernatural Book

What can be said about a book that has been shown time and again to predict the future? If we are intellectually honest, we are forced to conclude that it is from beyond this world for only God can predict the future in advance.

It is impossible to explain away the large body of prophetic passages in the Bible. The clarity of these prophecies and the accuracy of their fulfillment should not come as a surprise to those familiar with the Old Testament, for God says through the prophet Isaiah:

I am God, and there is no one like Me, declaring the end from the beginning, and from ancient times things which have not been done...(Isaiah 46:9-10)

God says there is no one like Him who can declare how things will turn out long before the events occur. God is in the business of foretelling the future. This is critical in understanding

Earth To Eternity

the divine nature of the Bible. Consider the following simple logic:

Premise 1:   Only God knows the future in clear detail.
Premise 2:   The Bible accurately predicts the future in clear detail.
Conclusion: Therefore, the Bible is from God.

It is clear that any book from God should be very carefully studied.

An Amazing Find in the Dead Sea Caves

As noted earlier, the critics of the Bible often claim that some of the books of the Bible were written much later than Bible scholars claim. The Book of Isaiah confounds the skepticism of the critics. The Book of Isaiah is one of the most important books of the Bible and it was written about 700 years before the birth of Jesus Christ. While we do not have the original scroll of Isaiah, a complete copy which dates to well before the birth of Christ has been found! During the 1940's, one of the greatest archaeological discoveries of modern times was made in the caves at Qumran near the Dead Sea. Initial discoveries were made by Bedouins, but soon archaeological expeditions were organized and the discoveries multiplied to include thousands of fragments of every Old Testament book except Esther. It was called "the greatest manuscript discovery of all time" by renowned archaeologist William Albright.[28]

The Dead Sea Scrolls are the remnants of the library of the ancient Essenes, a devout Jewish sect that once inhabited the monastery at Qumran well before the time of Christ. Among the ancient scrolls found at Qumran was a complete copy of all 66 chapters of the Old Testament Book of Isaiah which has been dated to about 100 B.C. or earlier. Astonishingly, this ancient parchment is virtually identical to other more recent Hebrew copies of Isaiah from which English Bible translations come, even though it predates these by a thousand years! This remarkable accuracy of reproduction of the Book of Isaiah over a 1,000 year period speaks to the reliability of the work of the scribes and copyists of the Old Testament. Moreover, it

The Bible: A Divine Book—Messianic Prophecy
invalidates the skepticism of Bible critics.[29, 30]

The most important thing about the Isaiah scroll found at Qumran is that it is filled with prophecies about the Messiah that were fulfilled in the Life of Jesus Christ, and it clearly demonstrates that these prophecies were written well before the birth of Christ! Over twenty characteristics of the Messiah, or events in his life were predicted in the Book of Isaiah alone. All were fulfilled in the life of Jesus Christ.

Prophecies About the Messiah in the Book of Isaiah		
Passage from Isaiah	New Testament Fulfillment	Nature of Prophecy
7:14	Mt. 1:23	He will be born of a virgin
11:1; 10	Mt. 1:1	He will be of the Davidic line
28:16	Ro. 9:32-3; 10:11	He is the cornerstone of the foundation
42:1	Mt. 3:15-7	He will have the Lord's Spirit upon Him and the Lord will uphold Him
49:7; 53:1-3	John 12:37	He will be rejected by Israel and the nations
42:6; 49:6	Mt. 28:18-20 Acts 1:7-8	He will extend salvation to the end of the earth and be a light to the Gentiles
50:4-5	Mt. 26:39	He will be obedient to the Lord
50:6	Mt. 27:26, 30	He will give His back to be struck, His beard to be plucked, and His face to be spit upon
52:14	Mt. 27:27-30	He will be disfigured by torture and cruelty
53:1-3	Mark 15:29-32	He will be despised and rejected by men
53:4-6	Mark 15:25	He will be stricken and afflicted for our sins
53:5-6	Ro. 4:25	He will be a sin offering
53:5	John 19:23 Luke 22:33	He will be pierced for our transgressions
53:7	Mt. 27:13-14	He will not speak to defend Himself
53:9	Mt. 27:56-60	He will be given a grave with the rich

It cannot be disputed that the Book of Isaiah found in modern Bibles comes from a text that was originally written before Jesus was born, and yet through prophecy, it describes

41

Earth To Eternity

many important events in His life! The table above summarizes the amazing record of prophecy and fulfillment in the Book of Isaiah, and once again confirms the supernatural origin of the Bible.

The Unity of the Bible—More Evidence of the Divine

The story the Bible spans the origin of humanity, the fall of humanity, the redemption of humanity, and the culmination of God's plan for humanity. What is striking is that the Bible was not written by a single author at a single time. Rather, it was written by about 40 authors, over a period of about 1,500 years, in different locations and languages, and in different literary styles. Yet it has amazing unity. Each author's contribution reveals part of the overall story, and it all fits together like tiles placed into a mosaic.

While the unity of the Bible does not prove the divine inspiration of it, it does suggest it. Think about it for a moment. How could the Bible convey such a unified story when it was written by many people, over many years, and in many places, unless it was coordinated in some way? I think the best answer is that God is the source of the Bible. That is why the story is unified. No human lived long enough to coordinate the storyline. If it is not of man, it must be of God, for the unity of the Bible could certainly not be an accident.

The Influence of the Bible

Consider the following observations of theologians Geisler and Nix:

No book has been more widely disseminated and has more broadly influenced the course of world events than the Bible. The Bible has been translated into more languages, been published in more copies, influenced more thought, inspired more art, and motivated more discoveries than any other book in history. The Bible has been translated into over one thousand languages representing more than ninety percent of the world's population. It has been published in billions of copies. There are no close seconds to it on the all-time bestseller list. The influence of the Bible and its teaching in the Western world is clear for all who study history. And the influential role of the West in the course of world events is equally clear. Civilization has been influenced more by the Judeo-Christian Scriptures than by any other book or series of books in the world. Indeed, no great moral or religious work in the world exceeds the depth of morality in the principle of Christian love, and none has a more lofty spiritual concept than the biblical view of God. The Bible presents the highest ideals known to men, ideals that have molded civilization.[31]

Could such a book be merely the product of human imagination? I think not.

Chapter 5
The New Testament: The Most Reliable Ancient Book

My goal in this chapter is to provide a synopsis of several lines of reasoning which I believe lead to the conclusion that the New Testament, which records Jesus' ministry, is a very reliable book.

Multiple Eyewitnesses of the Events

In assessing historical events, great weight is given to eyewitness testimony. Several factors tend to strengthen eyewitness testimony:

1. It is given soon after the events occurred before embellishment can occur.
2. It is provided by multiple independent witnesses to allow comparison of details.
3. It is given by neutral or hostile witnesses who have nothing to gain.
4. It contains details which are unfavorable to the witnesses since people generally do not make up things that make them look bad or weaken their position.[32]

All of the books included in the New Testament were written by eyewitnesses or their close associates. We know this through the writings of early church leaders and historians.

Matthew, Peter, and John were disciples of Jesus. Mark functioned as a scribe for Peter, and thus would have recorded Peter's eyewitness account of the New Testament events. Paul was a zealous persecutor of the church who converted to Christianity through a divine encounter with Jesus Christ on Damascus Road. Luke was a close associate of Paul. Although Luke was not an eyewitness to the resurrection, he was an eyewitness to Paul's ministry and miracles, and to the rapid growth of the early church. Most likely, Luke was acquainted with other eyewitnesses since he tells us at the beginning of his gospel that he carefully investigated everything from the beginning. James and Jude were half-brothers of Jesus (Jesus was fathered by God; James and Jude were fathered by Joseph).

Hebrews is an anonymous book, and may have been written by an eyewitness, but we cannot be certain. The writer of Hebrews was, at the very least, a person of great intellect who was in tune with the early church and its beliefs and doctrine.

The books selected for inclusion in the New Testament were all written before the close of the first century by the authors noted above. Other books surfaced in the second century such as the heretical Gnostic works discovered at Nag Hammadi in Egypt. These books were rejected by the early church because they lacked connection to the apostles who were eyewitnesses to the ministry of Jesus.

The New Testament Writers Were Reliable Eyewitnesses

In general, the factors described above that strengthen eyewitness testimony are clearly applicable to the New Testament authors. Within fifteen years after Jesus' resurrection, the New Testament books began to appear. With the exception of the Apostle John's books, and perhaps Jude's letter, it is likely the New Testament books were complete within 35 years of the resurrection. Some have contested early dates for the New Testament books, but noted scholar W. F. Albright concludes:

> In general, we can already say emphatically that there is no longer any solid basis for dating any book of the New Testament after about A.D. 80....[33]

This means that people who witnessed Jesus' ministry were still alive and would have been able to refute any embellishments to the true story.

As I will show in Chapter 7, the Apostles had nothing to gain by telling their story since in most cases they were put to gruesome deaths for proclaiming it. Paul started out completely hostile to Christianity and James was initially a skeptic.

Earth To Eternity

When we consider the New Testament, we find embarrassing details about the New Testament authors which enhance its credibility. After all, why would the authors write embarrassing things about themselves unless they were true? In the New Testament, we find John vying for position and power, Peter denying Christ three times before the rooster crows, and Paul as an accessory to murder.

The New Testament writers did not sugar coat Jesus' teachings about tough topics like hell, divorce, or morality which many would have found offensive. They also did not try to manage the collective story by harmonizing details, which they would have certainly done if they were trying to fabricate a hoax.

All of the above give the New Testament a ring of truth which can be heard by anyone willing to read it with an open mind.

Far More Early Manuscripts than Any Other Ancient Book

The New Testament was completed in the first century. While we do not have the original books, we do have a large amount of copies of the New Testament books. At present counting, nearly 6,000 fragments and partial and complete Greek manuscripts from the very early church survive to this day. These manuscripts are written on papyrus made from papyrus reeds, and on vellum and parchment which came from thin sections of animal hide. In addition to Greek manuscripts, there are about 9,000 early copies of the New Testament translated into Syriac, Coptic, Arabic and Latin, as well as other languages.[34]

The manuscript evidence for the New Testament is far better than for any book of the ancient world. Far more early copies of the New Testament exist than of any other ancient book. The New Testament manuscripts include fragments of the Gospel of John dating to about A.D. 130 and complete gospels of Luke and John dating to A.D. 200. Codex Sinaiticus contains the entire New Testament and has been dated to the fourth century, less than 300 years following the original writing of the New Testament. These are but a few of the early manuscripts of the thousands of New Testament manuscripts that survive to this day.

46

The New Testament: The Most Reliable Ancient Book

In contrast, ancient secular manuscripts have not fared so well. Only eight manuscripts each of *Thucydides's History* and *Herodotus's History* are still extant, yet they are considered among the most reliable historical works of the ancient world. The time gap between the writing of these histories and the available surviving manuscripts is about 1,300 years, yet they are accepted as fact virtually without question.[35]

The New Testament Was Accurately Transmitted

When multiple copies of ancient texts are available, it is easy to determine how well the text was preserved over time. Scholars merely look at the variation in different copies of the text as a function of time. By analyzing available manuscripts, scholars have concluded that the New Testament transmission accuracy is over 99 percent.

The majority of variations in the New Testament manuscripts are misspellings, omission of words, repetitions, reversal of letters, wrong division of words, etc. Given the vast number of manuscript copies, it is a straightforward task to reconstruct the original text of the New Testament with a high degree of confidence. None of the variations described affect in any way any of the basic beliefs or teachings of Christianity.

Manuscripts of the Ancient World[36]				
Author/ Book	Date Written	Earliest Copies	Time Gap	Number of Copies
Herodotus *History*	c. 484-425B.C.	A.D. 900	~1350 years	8
Thucydides *History*	c. 460-400 B.C.	A.D. 900	~1300 years	8
Plato	c. 400-350 B.C.	A.D. 900	~1300 years	20
Tacitus *Annals*	A.D. 100	A.D. 1100	~1000 years	20
New Testament	A.D. 50-100	A.D. 130-250	~50-150 years	5000+

The table above compares important books from the ancient world with respect to author, the date of writing of the original work, the date of writing of the earliest copies that have survived

47

to this day, the time gap elapsed between the writing of the original book and the earliest surviving copies, and the number of early copies surviving to this day.

As is easily seen from this table, there is far more manuscript evidence for the New Testament, in fact, the New Testament is in a class by itself in this regard.

The New Testament was carefully copied because the scribes who copied it believed it to be the Word of God. This has resulted in very high transmission accuracy. The net result is that the New Testament is the most well preserved and documented book of the ancient world. In support of this conclusion, Sir Frederic Kenyon, an eminent textual scholar and former Director and Principal Librarian of the British Museum wrote:

> The number of manuscripts of the New Testament, of early translations from it, and of quotations from it in the oldest writers of the Church, is so large that it is practically certain that the true reading of every doubtful passage is preserved in some one or other of these ancient authorities. This can be said of no other ancient book in the world.[37]

The New Testament Excels When Fact-Checked

A number of fact checking expeditions have been undertaken with respect to the New Testament to see if what it records is true. The result has been the confirmation at every turn of specific historical and geographical details cited in the New Testament.

The Book of Acts contains hundreds of specific details as would be expected in a factual eyewitness account. These include prevailing shipping winds, ports, titles of government officials, structure of the coastline, islands, cities, countries, landmarks, local industry, land routes, languages spoken in various places, political customs, and the rights of Roman citizens to name but a few. These have been cross-checked with other ancient sources, archaeological investigations, and local research. According to Norman Geisler, "Luke names thirty-two countries, fifty-four cities, and nine islands" without error.[38] Time and again, the Book of Acts has been vindicated.

One investigator of these matters was the prolific British

48

The New Testament: The Most Reliable Ancient Book
author, archaeologist, and New Testament scholar, Sir William Ramsay. He began his investigation of the Book of Acts with an unfavorable attitude toward it, but concluded in the end that it showed "marvelous truth."[39]

In a later book, Ramsay said this about Luke's stature as a historian:

> ...Luke is a historian of the first rank; not merely are his statements of fact; he is possessed of the true historic sense...this author should be placed along with the very greatest of historians.[40]

Similarly, Roman historian A. N. Sherwin-White affirms the wide acceptance of the reliability of the Book of Acts by Roman historians:

> For Acts the confirmation of historicity is overwhelming....Any attempt to reject its basic historicity must now appear absurd. Roman historians have long taken it for granted.[41]

Archaeology Supports the Accuracy of the New Testament

In the last one hundred years, archaeology has provided an immense amount of evidence in support of the Bible in general and the New Testament in particular. Many archaeological finds corroborate the facts presented in the New Testament. While archaeology cannot prove the New Testament, it can add important circumstantial evidence in support of it. The following is a partial list of archaeological discoveries that affirm specific facts presented in the New Testament:[42]

1. Structural remnants of Herod's Temple (John 2:20)
2. An inscription naming "Herod, King of Judea" (Matthew 2:1)
3. An inscription bearing the name and title, "Pontius Pilate, Prefect of Judea" (Luke 3:1)
4. A coin inscribed with the name Quirinius who ordered the census at the time of Jesus' birth (Luke 2:2)
5. A cave in Bethlehem long held to be the birthplace of Jesus (Luke 2:4-7)
6. The town of Capernaum on the shore of the Sea of Galilee, an important center of Jesus' ministry (Mark 2:1)
7. The house of the Apostle Peter in Capernaum (Matthew 8:14)

49

Earth To Eternity

8. The ossuary of Caiaphas, the high priest who condemned Jesus (Matthew 26:3)
9. Remains of a victim of crucifixion with a seven-inch nail remaining in his ankle bone (Acts 2:23)
10. The location of the crucifixion of Jesus and His place of burial (John 19:17; Mark 15:46)
11. The Pool of Siloam where Jesus performed a miraculous healing (John 9:1-12)
12. An inscription bearing the name "Erastus" mentioned by Paul in the Book of Romans (Romans 16:23)
13. The judgment seat where Paul stood before Gallio, Proconsul of Achaia (Acts 18:12)
14. The Pool of Bethsaida where Jesus healed a man who had been ill for thirty-eight years (John 5:1-5)
15. The Arch of Titus in the Roman forum which depicts the plunder of the temple after its destruction in A.D. 70 as prophesied by Jesus (Matthew 24:1-2)

Archaeology is a powerful witness to the plausibility of the New Testament as these specific examples show. I find the impressions of those who have spent decades digging in the Holy Land enlightening. Famed archaeologist of the Bible lands, Nelson Glueck, excavated over a 1,000 ancient sites. With respect to the agreement of archaeology with the Bible, he said this:

…It may be stated categorically that no archaeological discovery has ever controverted a Biblical reference. Scores of archaeological findings have been made which confirm in clear outline or in exact detail historical statements in the Bible.[43]

According to this eminent expert, no one has ever dug anything up that contradicted what the Bible says. Quite to the contrary, the Bible has been affirmed by scores of findings. How could this be unless the Bible is truly history?

A Great Legal Mind Affirms the Admissibility of the New Testament

Simon Greenleaf was one of the great legal minds of the nineteenth century. He was a law professor at Harvard and wrote *A Treatise On The Law of Evidences* which became a standard text for the training of lawyers.

The New Testament: The Most Reliable Ancient Book

Greenleaf was challenged to analyze the New Testament according to the standard methods for evaluating legal evidence. Greenleaf took on the challenge and produced an essay titled *Testimony of the Evangelists*. In it he concluded that according to the "Ancient Document Rule," the New Testament would be received into evidence as an authentic document since it bears no marks of forgery and has been in the proper custody of the church throughout the ages.

Greenleaf writes:

> The narratives of the evangelists are now submitted to the reader's perusal and examination, upon the principles and by the rules already stated....With the relative merits of modern harmonists, and with points of controversy among theologians the writer has no concern. His business is that of a lawyer examining the testimony of witnesses by the rules of his profession, in order to ascertain whether, if they had thus testified on oath, in a court of justice, they would be entitled to credit and whether their narratives, as we now have them, would be received as ancient documents, coming from the proper custody. If so, then it is believed that every honest and impartial man will act consistently with that result, by receiving their testimony in all the extent of its import.[44]

Greenleaf concludes here that the testimony of the evangelists is credible and should be accepted by "every honest and impartial" person.

Six
Jesus: Messiah, Miracle Worker, Son of God

The evidence for the reliability of New Testament narrative is substantial. It is difficult, given the evidence, not to take what it says about Jesus seriously.

The big question that must be answered is whether or not Jesus is the Son of God as Christianity claims. If He isn't, you don't have to worry about what He has to say. But if He is, as I believe the evidence will clearly show, then He knows some things the rest of us do not because His origin is with God in eternity. If Jesus is the Son of God, His words have great import and should carefully be studied and considered. A number of lines of reasoning lead us to the conclusion that Jesus is the Son of God.

I have organized the evidence into eight categories:

1. Jesus personally claimed to be the Messiah and the Son of God. His disciples affirmed this also.
2. Jesus fulfilled with stunning accuracy many of the Messianic prophecies. Those not yet fulfilled are appointed for fulfillment at Jesus' Second Coming.
3. Jesus was a miracle worker. The New Testament, which has been shown above to be the most reliable book of the ancient world, affirms His miraculous life.
4. Jesus rose from the dead.
5. The tomb Jesus was buried in was empty on the Sunday following His burial.
6. Christianity spread rapidly throughout the Roman Empire by peaceful means.
7. The claims of the early Christians about Jesus are affirmed by ancient secular, non-Christian sources.

8. Jesus is a unique person in history. There has never been anyone like Him in the history of the world.

Points 1, 2, and 3 will be considered in this chapter. Points 4, 5, and 6 will be considered in Chapter 7. Point 7 will be considered in Chapter 8. Point 8 will be addressed in Chapter 9.

For some, no amount of evidence will be convincing. For others, the weight of the evidence will be highly compelling when considered with an open mind. In my journey along this path, I could not explain away this body of evidence.

Jesus claimed to be God

I have heard it said by skeptics, "Jesus never claimed to be God, His followers just made that up after He died." The evidence is quite to the contrary. We learned earlier that the New Testament is the most reliable book of the ancient world. Consider what Jesus says about Himself in the New Testament.

In John 10:30, Jesus says that He is one with God: "I and the Father are one." In Mark 14:63-65, Jesus claims to be the Christ or the Messiah. The Jews understood that He was claiming to be God in the flesh, so they tried to kill Him:

> "...Are You the Christ, the Son of the Blessed One?" And Jesus said, "I am; and you shall see the Son of Man sitting at the right hand of Power, and coming with the clouds of heaven." Tearing his clothes, the high priest said, "What further need do we have of witnesses? You have heard the blasphemy; how does it seem to you?" And they all condemned Him to be deserving of death.

In a conversation with the Samaritan woman at the well, Jesus tells her plainly that He is the Messiah in John 4:24-26:

> "I know that Messiah is coming (He who is called Christ); when that One comes, He will declare all things to us." Jesus said to her, "I who speak to you am He."

Speaking to the religious leaders of His day, Jesus said:

> Truly, truly, I say to you, before Abraham was born, I am. (John 8:58)

Earth To Eternity

The only way Jesus could have existed before Abraham, who lived on earth over 2,000 years before Him, is if He were God.

Jesus clearly believed that He was God and He made that abundantly clear to other people.

Jesus' Disciples Believed that He Was God

Jesus' disciples recognized his divinity on a number of occasions. The Apostle Peter affirmed Jesus' divinity when Jesus asked Peter who he thought He was:

> Simon Peter answered, "You are the Christ, the Son of the living God." (Matthew 16:16)

Martha, the sister of Lazarus, responds to Jesus as follows:

> She said to Him, "Yes, Lord; I have believed that you are the Christ, the Son of God, even He who comes into the world." (John 11:27)

Sending a message down through the ages, The Apostle John says that he wrote his gospel so that *you* would believe that Jesus is the Son of God:

> Therefore many other signs Jesus also performed in the presence of the disciples, which are not written in this book; but these have been written so that you may believe that Jesus is the Christ, the Son of God; and that believing you may have life in His name." (John 20:30-31)

Those who followed Jesus during His life believed He was the Son of God. Information provided in the appendix shows that those who led the church after the Apostles also believed that Jesus was God.

Jesus Fulfilled the Messianic Prophecies

Among the most compelling evidence that Jesus is the Son of God is His astonishing fulfillment of the Messianic Prophecies. Jesus fulfilled many of the prophecies about the Messiah at His first coming as described in Chapter 4. Those that

Jesus: Messiah, Miracle Worker, Son of God

are unfulfilled at this time will be fulfilled at His future Second Coming which He promised.

As noted earlier, one physicist has estimated the probability that a single person could fulfill just forty-eight of the messianic prophecies is one chance in 10^{157}. This is, of course, an incredibly small probability.[45] The number 10^{157} is a *one* followed by 157 zeros! It is easy for us to understand probabilities of one chance in 100, or, one in a thousand. But one chance in 10^{157} is completely out of our experience. Suffice it to say that the chances of one person in the entire history of the world fulfilling all of the messianic prophecies is virtually zero...unless the events were orchestrated by some outside agent, which in this case would have to be God. Given Jesus' fulfillment of all of the Messianic prophecies against tremendous odds, it is difficult to see why so many do not recognize His identity. Jesus must truly be the Messiah, God in the flesh—the probabilities compel us in that direction.

Jesus' Miracles Further Prove His Divinity

The New Testament, which has been shown to be reliable, documents the many miracles performed by Jesus. It is important to remember that the New Testament authors had nothing to gain by claiming that Jesus performed miracles, as will be shown later. Have you heard any stories about the great wealth and power amassed by Matthew, John, Peter, Paul, and the rest? I am sure you haven't because there aren't any. Being a Christian in the first couple of centuries was not a good career move.

The New Testament includes eyewitness accounts of about 35 instantaneous miracles performed by Jesus, often before hundreds of watching people. The New Testament tells us that Jesus healed the sick and the blind, controlled natural forces, and was able to raise people from the dead. Jesus was able to turn water into wine and to feed thousands with a few loaves and fishes. As amazing as these miracles seem, they were easy for the Son of God. The Apostle John tells us in his gospel that everything that exists was created through Jesus, so healing sick people, or controlling the natural forces that He had created would not have been a big challenge for Him.

One such miracle was raising a dead man. Before raising

Earth To Eternity

Lazarus who had been dead for four days, Jesus said to Martha, one of Lazarus's sisters, "I am the resurrection and the life; he who believes in Me will live even if he dies."[46]

Jesus prayed and commanded Lazarus to come out of his tomb. The New Testament records the following account:

> Jesus said, "Remove the stone." Martha, the sister of the deceased, said to Him, "Lord, by this time there will be a stench, for he has been dead four days." Jesus said to her, "Did I not say to you that if you believe, you will see the glory of God?" So they removed the stone. Then Jesus raised His eyes, and said, "Father, I thank You that You have heard Me. I knew that You always hear Me; but because of the people standing around I said it, so that they may believe that You sent Me." When He had said these things, He cried out with a loud voice, "Lazarus, come forth." The man who had died came forth, bound hand and foot with wrappings, and his face was wrapped around with a cloth. Jesus said to them, "Unbind him, and let him go." (John 11:39-44)

Jesus did this amazing miracle to show that He was sent by God. Jesus changed many hearts and minds that day. The Apostle John goes on to say many of the Jews put their faith in Him after witnessing this great miracle. Only the Son of God, God in the flesh, could do such things.

Seven
The Truth of the Resurrection

The Evidence for the Resurrection of Jesus[47]

I don't think that many people would deny that if Jesus rose from the dead, then He must be God. There is very strong evidence that Jesus rose from the dead. This becomes clear when we consider the actions of the Apostles and Saul of Tarsus after the crucifixion of Jesus.

How should we proceed to prove or disprove events which occurred in the past? Some refuse to believe that Jesus rose from the dead because it is not scientifically reproducible. Like all events that have happened in the past, analyzing the truth of Christianity requires an evaluation of its claims using legal and historical methods.

The approach to assessing events of the past relies on forensic methods as opposed to scientific methods. Things that happened in the past cannot be proven scientifically because they cannot be recreated. For instance, we cannot prove scientifically that George Washington was the first president of the United States because we cannot recreate the Revolutionary period. But we can conclude beyond the shadow of a doubt that he was the first president by evaluating the eyewitness testimonies, documents, and archaeological evidence of that time. While we cannot speak to George Washington, we would give the greatest weight to his writings and other eyewitness accounts of the events surrounding his presidency. So let's consider the eyewitness testimony about the events surrounding Jesus' death, His resurrection, and the rise of the early church.

The Apostles Saw the Resurrected Jesus

The New Testament paints a grim picture of the Apostles

57

after the crucifixion of Jesus. The charismatic leader they had followed for three years had been put to an ignominious death—He was crucified like a common criminal—and those who followed Him were in fear for their own lives. The Apostle John writes of that time that the disciples were gathered together behind closed doors because of their fear of the Jews. They were afraid, no doubt, that they would be next. Unexpectedly Jesus appeared in the room where the disciples were assembled. John writes this:

> So when it was evening on that day, the first day of the week, and when the doors were shut where the disciples were, for fear of the Jews, Jesus came and stood in their midst and said to them, "Peace be with you." And when He had said this, He showed them both His hands and His side. The disciples then rejoiced when they saw the Lord. (John 20:19-20)

Jesus did not come to the disciples as a mere apparition. Luke indicates that Jesus challenged the disciples to touch Him. He ate a piece of broiled fish in their presence. He did these things to show that He was a being of flesh and blood and that He had truly risen from the dead (Luke 24:39-43).

With Jesus Dead, the Jews Sought To Take Back Control

With Jesus crucified, the Jews were seeking to reassert control of the people. The young Jewish zealot, Saul of Tarsus, was unleashed to persecute the followers of Jesus.

We meet Saul at the stoning of Stephen who was a follower of Jesus. Saul looked on with approval at the death of Stephen as Luke writes in the Book of Acts:

> Saul was in hearty agreement with putting him to death. And on that day a great persecution began against the church in Jerusalem, and they were all scattered throughout the regions of Judea and Samaria, except the apostles. Some devout men buried Stephen, and made loud lamentation over him. But Saul began ravaging the church, entering house after house, and dragging off men and women, he would put them in prison.(Acts 8:1-3)

Saul was about to have a life changing experience as we

58

The Truth of the Resurrection
will read below.

The Disciples Risked Their Lives to Proclaim the Resurrection

The early church grew rapidly in spite of persecution and hardship. Shortly after the death of Jesus on the cross, the apostles were boldly proclaiming the truth of the resurrection of Jesus.

On the day of Pentecost, which is considered to be the day the church was born, Peter spoke to a crowd of thousands of Jews from many nations in Jerusalem. Peter proclaimed the death and resurrection of Jesus. Luke records that on that day, about 3,000 people came to believe in Jesus (Luke 2).

Later, Peter and John were healing the sick in the temple and proclaiming that Jesus rose from the dead. Shortly thereafter, Peter and John were arrested by the Jews; Peter defended his actions before the Jewish leaders:

> Then Peter, filled with the Holy Spirit, said to them, "Rulers and elders of the people, if we are on trial today for a benefit done to a sick man, as to how this man has been made well, let it be known to all of you and to all the people of Israel, that by the name of Jesus Christ the Nazarene, whom you crucified, whom God raised from the dead—by this name this man stands here before you in good health. He is the stone which was rejected by you, the builders, but which became the chief corner stone. And there is salvation in no one else; for there is no other name under heaven that has been given among men by which we must be saved." (Acts 4:8-12)

The Jews were at a loss as to what to do. They commanded the apostles not to speak or teach in the name of Jesus, but the apostles continued to do it anyway. The apostles, disciples, and those who came to believe in Jesus, proclaimed the truth of the resurrection and many were killed for doing so. According to secular writings, early church writings, and the Bible, this is how some of the apostles and disciples of Jesus died:[48]

Stephen	Stoned
Paul	Beheaded
Peter	Crucified
James (Jesus' brother)	martyred

59

Earth To Eternity

James	Cut with a sword
Thomas	Pierced with a spear
Philip	Crucified
Bartholomew	Crucified
Andrew	Crucified
Many Others	Burned as human torches, crucified, or ripped to shreds by wild animals under Nero

What could have caused this transformation in the demoralized apostles and disciples who had just seen their leader put to death? What could have caused a transformation so complete that the apostles and disciples of Jesus were prepared to die in order to continue proclaiming the resurrection? *The only reasonable answer is that the apostles and disciples truly believed that they had seen the resurrected Christ.* It really doesn't make sense that the apostles and disciples would keep on saying something that was likely to lead to their death unless they really believed that it was true!

The Conversion of James, the Half-Brother of Jesus

Joseph and Mary apparently had children after Jesus was born. The New Testament tells us that Jesus had brothers (Matthew 13:55; Mark 6:3). They would be Jesus' half-brothers because they had a different father than Jesus. Jesus was conceived by the Holy Spirit; Jesus' other siblings were presumably conceived by Joseph.

Jesus was the first born and James was Jesus' oldest brother. Luke's and John's gospels tell us that Jesus' brothers, at first, did not believe in Him (Luke 8:19–21; John 7:5). Like many others, they were skeptical. For James, something obviously happened to overcome that skepticism.

In his letters, Paul indicates that the resurrected Jesus appeared to James.[49] James became a believer in Jesus, a missionary, and the leader of the church in Jerusalem. James was ultimately put to death by the Jewish leaders in Jerusalem for proclaiming the truth of the resurrection of Jesus. What can possibly account for this change in James's attitude? *The only reasonable answer is that James truly believed that he had seen the resurrected Christ.*

60

The Truth of the Resurrection

Paul Changes From Chief Persecutor to Chief Evangelist

Saul of Tarsus was the zealous and ambitious Jew we encountered above in the stoning of Stephen. We encounter Saul again in the Book of Acts where he is on a crusade to wipe out believers in Jesus:

> Now Saul, still breathing threats and murder against the disciples of the Lord, went to the high priest, and asked for letters from him to the synagogues at Damascus, so that if he found any belonging to the Way, both men and women, he might bring them bound to Jerusalem. (Acts 9:1-2)

Saul was rounding up those belonging to the "Way," an early name for Christianity, to bring them back to Jerusalem for trial. We learn elsewhere that Saul was an up and coming Jew, trained in Jerusalem by a leading rabbi. While Saul was on the road going to Damascus, Syria, he had a life changing experience:

> As he was traveling, it happened that he was approaching Damascus, and suddenly a light from heaven flashed around him; and he fell to the ground and heard a voice saying to him, "Saul, Saul, why are you persecuting Me?" And he said, "Who are You, Lord?" And He said, "I am Jesus whom you are persecuting, but get up and enter the city, and it will be told you what you must do." The men who traveled with him stood speechless, hearing the voice but seeing no one. Saul got up from the ground, and though his eyes were open, he could see nothing; and leading him by the hand, they brought him into Damascus. (Acts 9:1-8)

According to the Book of Acts, Saul encountered the resurrected Jesus. Saul would later become the Apostle Paul, the greatest Christian evangelist of all time. Paul confirms in his own writings that the resurrected Jesus appeared to him (1 Corinthians 15:8).

After this life changing event, Paul recounts the persecution he endured to continue proclaiming the resurrection of Jesus:

> Five times I received from the Jews thirty-nine lashes. Three times I was beaten with rods, once I was stoned, three times I was shipwrecked, a night and a day I have spent in the deep. I have

Earth To Eternity

been on frequent journeys, in dangers from rivers, dangers from robbers, dangers from my countrymen, dangers from the Gentiles, dangers in the city, dangers in the wilderness, dangers on the sea, dangers among false brethren; I have been in labor and hardship, through many sleepless nights, in hunger and thirst, often without food, in cold and exposure. Apart from such external things, there is the daily pressure on me of concern for all the churches. (2 Corinthians 11:24-28)

Paul suffered throughout his life because he refused to stop proclaiming the truth of the resurrection of Jesus. That put him at odds with the Jews and the Romans who did not understand or believe in Christianity. In the end, he was beheaded during Nero's persecution of Christians.

What could account for Paul's willingness to continually risk death and bring suffering upon himself in order to proclaim the resurrection of Jesus? *The only reasonable answer is that Paul truly believed that he had seen the resurrected Christ on the road to Damascus.*

Jesus Rose from the Dead: The Events of History Affirms It

Why would the apostles and disciples be willing to die proclaiming the truth of the resurrection? Why would Jesus' skeptical half-brother become the leader of the church in Jerusalem and ultimately die for his beliefs? Why would Saul of Tarsus change from chief persecutor of the church to its chief evangelist, the Apostle Paul, traveling tens of thousands of miles, suffering beatings, whipping, stoning, shipwreck, and near drowning? None of Jesus' followers gained anything but persecution for their deeds. The New Testament is clear that Jesus' followers were not rich in worldly possessions.

The only answer that makes sense is that all of these individuals truly believed that they had encountered the resurrected Christ. Who would risk their life to die for a lie? There was certainly no fame or fortune to be had in proclaiming the resurrection—only persecution and death!

The events of the first century cannot be easily explained away. Peter, John, Matthew, Paul, John, James and the other apostles and disciples believed they saw the resurrected Christ, and went to their deaths proclaiming it. *Jesus' followers believed*

The Truth of the Resurrection

in the resurrection and their actions proved it. This is the best explanation for the change seen in the apostles and disciples.

Paul affirms that many saw the resurrected Christ in his first letter to the Corinthians:

> For I delivered to you as of first importance what I also received, that Christ died for our sins according to the Scriptures, and that He was buried, and that He was raised on the third day according to the Scriptures, and that He appeared to Cephas [Aramaic name of Peter], then to the twelve. After that He appeared to more than five hundred brethren at one time, most of whom remain until now, but some have fallen asleep; then He appeared to James, then to all the apostles; and last of all, as to one untimely born, He appeared to me also. (1 Corinthians 15:3-8)

Paul is saying here, Christ died for our sins; he was buried, and rose from the dead after three days. Then He appeared to Peter and the apostles, to over 500 of Jesus' disciples at once, to James, and finally to Paul. Paul says many of those who saw Jesus were still alive at the time of his writing, as if to say, "Go and check it out for yourselves. Talk to the witnesses yourselves." Why would Paul write these things (that could easily be contradicted if false) unless they were true? Over 500 people could not have suffered the same exact delusion. The only sensible answer is he did it because it was true. *Jesus really did rise from the dead and was witnessed by many.*

Only God Could Rise from the Dead

If Jesus rose from the dead as the evidence clearly indicates, then Jesus is the Son of God as He claimed. It would be ill advised to ignore, dismiss, or reject the Son of God.

Jesus Rose from the Dead: The Empty Tomb Affirms It

The Jews' reaction to the events surrounding the resurrection shows that the tomb was really empty on that Sunday morning after the crucifixion and burial of Jesus.

We know the tomb was empty because the Jewish leaders had to make up a story that the body had been stolen by Jesus' disciples. If the body was still in the tomb, they would not have had to make up a story explaining it away!

Earth To Eternity

Matthew's gospel documents the reaction of the Jewish leaders:

> Now while they were on their way, some of the guard came into the city and reported to the chief priests all that had happened. And when they had assembled with the elders and consulted together, they gave a large sum of money to the soldiers, and said, "You are to say, 'His disciples came by night and stole Him away while we were asleep.' And if this should come to the governor's ears, we will win him over and keep you out of trouble." And they took the money and did as they had been instructed; and this story was widely spread among the Jews, and is to this day. (Matthew 28:11-15)

The bottom line is the tomb was empty on that first Easter morning.[50] What about the possibility that Jesus' disciples stole away the His body? In Matthew 27, we learn that the Jews had posted a guard at Jesus' grave and set a seal upon it. The grave was secure which is why they needed to pay off the guards to say that Jesus' body was stolen by His disciples while they slept.

The body of Jesus either was hidden, disappeared into thin air, or as the disciples of Jesus tell us, Jesus rose from the dead and walked out of the tomb. The disciples did not have an opportunity to steal Jesus' body, the tomb was guarded. Nor did they have anything to gain by doing so. Jesus' body obviously did not disappear into thin air. There is no ancient evidence that Jesus' body was discovered, but there is ample evidence that Jesus rose from the dead as was discussed in detail above. It seems most reasonable to accept the disciples' account of the resurrection given their actions and willingness to die for their claims.

Evidence of the Rapid Spread of Christianity

The Apostles and the disciples of Jesus spread the news about the resurrection of Jesus rapidly throughout the Roman world. By the end of the second century, Christianity had spread 2,500 miles from Jerusalem in an age when travel was by foot, sailing vessel, or on the back of an animal.

In less than two centuries, Christian communities were established around the Mediterranean world in what are now

Israel, Turkey, Bulgaria, Greece, Italy, France, Germany, Britain, Spain, Algiers, Tunisia, Libya, and Egypt.[51]

The disciples spread the news because Jesus had told them to go and make disciples of all nations, baptizing them in the name of the Father, Son, and Holy Spirit just before He ascended into heaven:

> And Jesus came up and spoke to them, saying, "All authority has been given to Me in heaven and on earth. "Go therefore and make disciples of all the nations, baptizing them in the name of the Father and the Son and the Holy Spirit, teaching them to observe all that I commanded you; and lo, I am with you always, even to the end of the age." (Matthew 28:18-20)

Jesus had promised eternal life to all who believed in Him, but only to those who believed in Him. Jesus says in John 3:16-18:

> For God so loved the world, that He gave His only begotten Son, that whoever believes in Him shall not perish, but have eternal life. For God did not send the Son into the world to judge the world, but that the world might be saved through Him. He who believes in Him is not judged; he who does not believe has been judged already, because he has not believed in the name of the only begotten Son of God. (John 3:16-18)

Clearly, the apostles and disciples acted in a way that shows that they believed Jesus' instructions and the importance of getting that message out, even if it cost them their lives.

It is important to note that this rapid early spread of Christianity was accomplished by completely peaceful means and at much personal risk. Much of the persecution of the early Christians came to an end when the Roman Emperor Constantine the Great issued the Edict of Milan in A.D. 313 legalizing Christian worship, thus allowing the spread of Christianity to accelerate.

Eight
Ancient Non-Christian Writings Affirm Christian Claims

It is not unusual to hear someone say that nothing is known about Jesus outside of the New Testament or that He never existed. The fact is that a number of ancient sources outside of the Bible affirm the important claims of Christianity. *I am not saying that secular writers believed that Jesus was the Son of God and that He rose from the dead, but they do affirm that these things were being said about Him in the first and second century.*

I will end this chapter with a summary of what we learn from ancient secular and non-Christian writings about Christianity, but first, let's consider the writings themselves.

Tacitus

Tacitus, a Roman historian writing in A.D. 109, affirms the torture of Christians during Nero's reign. It seems that Nero was suspected by some of setting the great fire of Rome. To deflect the blame from himself, Nero blamed the Christians as scapegoats. Christus (Latin form of Christ), is identified as the originator of Christianity who was killed by Pontius Pilate. Tacitus indicates that the early Christians were killed in excruciating manners. They were torn by dogs, crucified, or burnt as human torches to provide illumination at night. Nero reigned from A.D. 54 to A.D. 68. The great fire of Rome occurred in A.D. 64, so this persecution of Christians broke out toward the end of Nero's reign. It is during this period that the Apostles Peter and Paul are thought to have been martyred. Tacitus writes this gruesome account in the following passage from *Annals*:

66

Ancient Non-Christian Writings Affirm Christian Claims

Consequently, to get rid of the report, Nero fastened the guilt and inflicted the most exquisite tortures on a class hated for their abominations, called Christians by the populace. Christus, from whom the name had its origin, suffered the extreme penalty during the reign of Tiberius at the hands of one of our procurators, Pontius Pilatus, and a most mischievous superstition, thus checked for the moment, again broke out not only in Judaea, the first source of the evil, but even in Rome, where all things hideous and shameful from every part of the world find their centre and become popular. Accordingly, an arrest was first made of all who pleaded guilty; then, upon their information, an immense multitude was convicted, not so much of the crime of firing the city, as of hatred against mankind. Mockery of every sort was added to their deaths. Covered with the skins of beasts, they were torn by dogs and perished, or were nailed to crosses, or were doomed to the flames and burnt, to serve as a nightly illumination, when daylight had expired.[52]

Josephus

Josephus was a first century Jewish historian who lived from A.D. 37 or 38 to A.D. 97. He served in the Roman army, and later in his career, he was appointed as court historian under the Roman Emperor Vespasian. Josephus wrote the following in *Antiquites*:

At this time there was a wise man who was called Jesus. His conduct was good and [he] was known to be virtuous. And many people from among the Jews and the other nations became his disciples. Pilate condemned him to be crucified and to die. But those who became his disciples did not abandon his discipleship. They reported that he had appeared to them three days after his crucifixion, and that he was alive; accordingly he was perhaps the Messiah, concerning whom the prophets have recounted wonders.[53]

Josephus informs us that Jesus was a wise and virtuous man who garnered a significant following. He was sentenced to crucifixion by Pilate, but even after He died, His disciples continued to follow His teaching and claimed that they had seen Him. Josephus, a Jew who would have been familiar with the prophecies, goes so far as to say "perhaps" He was the Messiah predicted by the prophets.

67

Thallus

Thallus wrote around A.D. 52. None of his works are still in existence, though a few fragmented citations are preserved by other writers. One such writer is Julius Africanus who wrote in about A.D. 221. He cites Thallus regarding the events surrounding the crucifixion of Christ. Thallus describes an eclipse and an earthquake at the time of the crucifixion of Christ:

> On the whole world there pressed a most fearful darkness; and the rocks were rent by an earthquake, and many places in Judea and other districts were thrown down. This darkness Thallus, in the third book of his *History*, calls, as appears to me without reason, an eclipse of the sun.[54]

In this passage, Julius Africanus, citing Thallus, affirms that after the crucifixion, darkness came upon the world of the type associated with an eclipse, even though an eclipse was not expected, and that an earthquake occurred. Thus Thallus, writing less than twenty years after the crucifixion, confirms events described by the gospel writers, Mathew and Luke (Mt. 27:51; Luke 23:44).

Pliny the Younger and Emperor Trajan in A.D. 112

Pliny the Younger was a Roman administrator. He was the adopted son of Pliny the Elder, a natural historian. Pliny the Younger held several military and civil positions including imperial magistrate under the Roman Emperor Trajan.

In the following passage, Pliny seeks the advice of Trajan with respect to the handling of Christians. In this exchange, we learn that Christians were persecuted for practicing devotion to Christ.

The Roman policy at that time was to offer Christians an opportunity to recant, curse Christ, and to worship the Roman gods and the emperor. If they were willing to do this, they would be pardoned and set free. Otherwise they were to be punished. We learn that true Christian believers would not curse the name of Christ and worship the Roman gods.

This passage also provides insight into early Christian worship: on a fixed day, Christians would meet to offer hymns to

Ancient Non-Christian Writings Affirm Christian Claims

Christ whom they reverenced as God. They agreed to refrain from evil and then departed. Later, Christians would assemble for a fellowship meal.

Trajan, in his response, affirms Pliny's handling of Christians.

Pliny's Question to Trajan:

It is my custom, Sire, to refer to you in all cases where I am in doubt, for who can better clear up difficulties and inform me? I have never been present at any legal examination of the Christians, and I do not know, therefore, what are the usual penalties passed upon them, or the limits of those penalties, or how searching an inquiry should be made.... In the meantime, this is the plan which I have adopted in the case of those Christians who have been brought before me. I ask them whether they are Christians, if they say "Yes," then I repeat the question the second time, and also a third – warning them of the penalties involved; and if they persist, I order them away to prison. For I do not doubt that – be their admitted crime what it may – their pertinacity and inflexible obstinacy surely ought to be punished....Those who denied that they were or had been Christians and called upon the gods with the usual formula, reciting the words after me, and those who offered incense and wine before your image—which I had ordered to be brought forward for this purpose, along with the regular statues of the gods – all such I considered acquitted – especially as they cursed the name of Christ, which it is said *bona fide* Christians cannot be induced to do.[55]

Pliny continues to describe Christian worship as he understands it:

... on a fixed day they used to meet before dawn and recite a hymn among themselves to Christ, as though he were a god. So far from binding themselves by oath to commit any crime, they swore to keep from theft, robbery, adultery, breach of faith, and not to deny any trust money deposited with them when called upon to deliver it. This ceremony over, they used to depart and meet again to take food – but it was of no special character, and entirely harmless.[56]

Trajan's reply to Pliny:

You have adopted the right course, my dear Pliny, in examining the cases of those cited before you as Christians; for no hard and fast rule can be laid down covering such a wide question. The

Earth To Eternity

Christians are not to be hunted out. If brought before you, and the offense is proved, they are to be punished, but with this reservation -- if any one denies he is a Christian, and makes it clear he is not, by offering prayer to our gods, then he is to be pardoned on his recantation, no matter how suspicious his past.[57]

Lucian of Samosata (c. A.D. 125-A.D. 180)

Lucian of Samosata was an Assyrian satirist who wrote in the Greek language. In the passage below, we learn that Christians in his day worshipped Christ who was the originator of Christianity. We also learn that the Christians regarded themselves to be immortal, and for this reason, they were not afraid of death. They regarded each other as brothers, denied the Greek gods, and worshipped Christ who had been crucified. They were not attached to worldly goods and considered their property to be in common.

The Christians, you know, worship a *man* to this day,--the distinguished personage who introduced their novel rites, and was crucified on that account....You see, these misguided creatures start with the general conviction that they are immortal for all time, which explains the contempt of death and voluntary self-devotion which are so common among them; and then it was impressed on them by their original lawgiver that they are all brothers, from the moment that they are converted, and deny the gods of Greece, and worship the crucified sage, and live after his laws. All this they take quite on trust, with the result that they despise all worldly goods alike, regarding them merely as common property.[58]

A Jewish Source: The Babylonian Talmud

An early Jewish source regarding the execution of Jesus (Yeshu) is found in the Babylonian Talmud in the records of the Sanhedrin. This passage dates to the first two centuries and tells us that the Jews announced their plans to stone Jesus in advance. In the end, we learn that Jesus was hanged, as in "hanged on a tree," another expression referring to crucifixion used by the Apostle Peter in Acts 5:30. We learn that Jesus was accused of sorcery, which would speak to His ability to do miracles. It is also clear that the Sanhedrin was concerned that Jesus was

Ancient Non-Christian Writings Affirm Christian Claims

leading people away from their control into what they termed as "apostasy." This passage further confirms that Jesus was executed on the eve of the Passover as is reported in the gospels.

> On the eve of the Passover Yeshu was hanged. For forty days before the execution took place, a herald went forth and cried, "He is going forth to be stoned because he has practiced sorcery and enticed Israel to apostacy [sic]. Any one who can say anything in his favour, let him come forward and plead on his behalf." But since nothing was brought forward in his favour he was hanged on the eve of Passover![59]

Non-Christian Sources Affirm the Major Claims of Christianity

As I said at the beginning of this chapter, the major claims of Christianity are affirmed by secular and non-Christian writers. That is not to say that the claims were believed by the secular and Jewish writers, but it is clear that the major claims of Christianity in the twenty-first century were present in the first and second century.

We can summarize what is learned about early Christianity from these sources as follows: 1) Christians were persecuted and martyred for their beliefs. 2) True Christians refused to recant their testimony about Jesus. 3) Early Christians followed Jesus' teaching and were willing to die for their beliefs. 4) Jesus worked wonders or amazing signs which were interpreted by some as sorcery. 5) Christianity spread rapidly in the Roman world. 6) Christians were peaceful. 7) Christians refused to worship the Roman and Greek gods. 8) Christians believed that Jesus rose from the dead. 8) Christians believed that they would have eternal life. 9) Jesus led a virtuous life. 10) Many Jews and Gentiles became followers of Jesus. 11) Jesus was condemned to die and was crucified by Pontius Pilate. 12) Jesus appeared to the disciples three days after His death.

The secular and Jewish writers add significant validation to the reports that are made in the New Testament.

Christians Refused to Recant—More Evidence for the Resurrection

By the second century, Christianity was spreading rapidly. As we learned above from the correspondence between Pliny and the Roman Emperor Trajan in A.D. 112, Christians who recanted their testimony about Jesus and venerated the Roman gods could be pardoned. Yet true Christians went to their death refusing to renounce Jesus and the truth of His resurrection. Often these Christians would suffer torture for days, but in the end, their refusal to renounce Jesus ended in horrific deaths. Many were crucified, burned at the stake, or fed to wild animals.

The Christians in the early first century were in a position to know if the major claims of Christianity were true. They needed only to inquire of those from the previous generation, parents and grandparents, who were in a position to be eyewitnesses to the events. Would anyone doubt a parent's or a grandparent's recollection of the events he or she witnessed in World War II? Certainly most would trust their parents and grandparents just as the early Christians would trust their parents and grandparents. If Christianity and its central claims about Jesus were a lie, the early Christians would have known it, renounced it, denied Jesus, and worshipped the Roman gods to save their lives—but they didn't do it!

No one will die for something that they know to be a lie. Early Christians refused to renounce Jesus and worship the Roman gods because they believed that Jesus really was the Son of God who rose from the dead, and that through faith in Him they gained the most important thing of all, eternal life in heaven. No earthly, temporal torment was worth sacrificing that!

Nine
The Unique Truth of Christianity

Jesus is Superior to all Other Religious Leaders

As part of the review for a world religions class I taught, I put together a summary of what makes Jesus different from Muhammad, Buddha, Confucius, the 330 million gods of the Hindus, and any other religious leader that has ever existed.

Jesus really is like no other religious leader because all of following things are true about Him, and I can find no credible evidence that they are true of any other religious leader who ever existed.

1. His coming and life were predicted hundreds of years in advance with many clear prophecies.
2. He fulfilled all of the prophecies about His life.
3. He led a sinless life.
4. He performed miracles which were witnessed by many.
5. He predicted the future, some of which has already been fulfilled.
6. His story is told in a book (the Bible) that can be demonstrated to be of divine origin.
7. He gave His life as a ransom for many.
8. He rose from the dead.
9. He said that He was God and He proved it.
10. He promised to return.
11. He said that He personally was the source of eternal life.
12. He described a heaven that is far beyond human experience.

73

Earth To Eternity

Not a single one of these things is true about any individual that ever existed in the history of the world except Jesus! Jesus is truly unique! He transcends this earthly realm and is therefore able to grant us access to the heavenly realm.

Christianity: The One True Religion

Is it possible that all religions are true? The answer is no, because all religions contradict each other. Consider the table below.

Comparison of Major Belief Systems					
Claim	Atheist	Muslim	Jew	Christian	New Age/ Eastern Religion
Jesus is the unique Son of God	No	No	No	Yes	No
Man is God	No	No	No	No	Yes
There is No God	Yes	No	No	No	No
Muhammad is the greatest prophet	No	Yes	No	No	No

A quick glance at this table reveals that there is much disagreement in the world's belief systems. Only Christians would answer in the affirmative that Jesus is the one and only Son of God. Atheists don't believe in God, Muslims don't believe that God can have a Son, and Jews certainly deny this. New Agers/Eastern religion practitioners might see Jesus as an enlightened being or an avatar, but not the unique Son of God.

Only New Agers see man as God, in fact, a significant focus of New Age religions is attaining the self-awareness of one's own godhood.

Of course, only atheism would affirm that there is no God; however, certain forms of Buddhism tend toward atheism.

Only Muslims would affirm that Muhammad is the final and greatest prophet.

We have quickly come to the conclusion that world religions contradict each other in many ways, yet each implicitly claims to be the ultimate truth.

The Unique Truth of Christianity

Christianity claims that Jesus is the Son of God, who rose from the dead. All other belief systems deny this claim. In a courtroom, if two witnesses contradict each other, either one is lying and the other is telling the truth, or both witnesses are lying. The same can be said of world religions. At most, only one religion can be the true. It is also logically possible that all religions are false.

How Do We Know Which Religion is True, if Any?

The question that should be asked is, "Which religion's truth claims are supported by historical, archaeological, and prophetic evidence, and which religion has the marks of supernatural origin?"

In my fairly extensive study of this issue, I am not aware of any credible supporting evidence for the truth claims of other world religions of the type presented in the previous chapters for Christianity. Christianity is truly unique in that regard. You needn't take my word for it. You can conduct your own private study of world religions.

Jesus claims to be the only way to God saying "I am the way, and the truth, and the life; no one comes to the Father but through Me." (John 14:6)

Is Jesus really the Son of God and the only way to God? I hope that the evidence presented in the preceding chapters has made the answer is obvious.

Ten
What Jesus and the Apostles Taught About the Bible

I hope you will agree that there is a considerable amount of evidence that the Bible is from God and that Jesus is the Messiah, the Son of God. If Jesus is truly divine, we should pay careful attention to what He teaches. In particular, let's consider what Jesus taught about the Bible.

Jesus' View of the Bible

In the following passage, Jesus affirms the imperishability of the "Law and the Prophets" which is the entire Old Testament. He says that He came as the fulfillment of them, which certainly makes sense given that He fulfilled the Messianic prophecies. Moreover, Jesus says that not a single part or the smallest detail of the Old Testament will fail to be fulfilled as we learn below.

> Do not think that I came to abolish the Law or the Prophets; I did not come to abolish but to fulfill. For truly I say to you, until heaven and earth pass away, not the smallest letter or stroke shall pass from the Law until all is accomplished. (Matthew 5:17-18)

Jesus says that man needs more than food to live. Man also needs God's Word contained in the Bible :

> … It is written, 'Man shall not live on bread alone, but on every word that proceeds out of the mouth of God.' (Matthew 4:4)

Jesus says that the Scriptures, i.e. the Old Testament, is unbreakable, and further, Jesus equates God's Word with truth:

> … the Scripture cannot be broken…(John 10:35)

What Jesus and the Apostles Taught About the Bible
Sanctify them in the truth; your word is truth. (John 17:17)

Jesus rebukes the Sadducees and tells them that their mistakes come from not understanding the Old Testament Scriptures:

> But Jesus answered and said to them, "You are mistaken, not understanding the Scriptures nor the power of God. (Matthew 22:29)

Jesus promised to send the Holy Spirit to guide the Apostles "into all the truth," and thus He promised to inspire the New Testament:

> I have many more things to say to you, but you cannot bear them now. "But when He, the Spirit of truth, comes, He will guide you into all the truth; for He will not speak on His own initiative, but whatever He hears, He will speak; and He will disclose to you what is to come." (John 16:12-13)

Jesus, the Son of God who rose from the dead, confirmed that the entire Old Testament is the Word of God and promised that the New Testament would be guided by the Spirit of God. Therefore, from beginning to end, the Bible is the Word of God.
Consider the following simple logic:

Premise 1:   God cannot err
Premise 2:   Jesus taught that the Bible is the Word of God
Conclusion: Therefore, the Bible must be free of errors

The Apostle's View of the Bible

The Apostle Paul says, "All Scripture is inspired by God and profitable for teaching, for reproof, for correction, for training in righteousness." (2 Timothy 3:16) Moreover, Peter says, "But know this first of all, that no prophecy of scripture is a matter of one's own interpretation, for no prophecy was ever made by an act of human will, but men moved by the Holy Spirit spoke from God." (2 Peter 1:20-21) Later in this letter, Peter refers to Paul's letters as "Scripture" indicating that Paul's letters are inspired by God. (2 Peter 3:15-16)

77

Earth To Eternity

The Apostles Peter and Paul clearly taught that the Scriptures were given to us by God. The Scriptures are contained in the Bible and are God's infallible revelation to humanity, and are true in all that they affirm.

Eleven
What Christianity Teaches—A Simple Summary

Christianity teaches many things but here is a short list of some of the most important things made clear in the Bible:

1. The universe and everything in it was created by God through Jesus Christ.
2. Humans are separated from God because all have sinned.
3. Christ was born of the Virgin Mary.
4. Christ is the Son of God.
5. Christ died on a cross as payment for the sins of all people.
6. Christ rose from the dead.
7. By His sacrifice, Christ reconciled all who believe in Him to God.
8. All who repent and believe in Christ will be granted eternal life in heaven.
9. All who believe in Christ should be baptized in the name of the Father, Son, and Holy Spirit, and follow the teachings of Jesus.
10. The Bible (Old Testament and New Testament Scriptures) is the inspired, inerrant Word of God.
11. Christ will return at the Second Coming.
12. The destiny of all humans is heaven or hell.

What is True Christianity?

True Christianity teaches what the Bible teaches, because it is the inspired Word of God, without error (see Chapters 3, 4, 5 and 10). In short, Christians believe that everything the Bible affirms is true. Christians view the Bible as the ultimate guide for understanding and living life. God, working through the Holy

Spirit, used ordinary people (the prophets), having distinct personalities, to convey His message to humanity through the ages. This resulted in the compilation of the Bible.

As was discussed previously, Christians believe the Bible is the Word of God for several important reasons.

1. The Bible contains many detailed prophecies concerning the Messiah, Israel, people, and nations which have been fulfilled literally in the history of the world, as has been shown above.
2. Archaeology has provided resounding support for the history and peoples presented in the Bible.
3. The Bible is supported by early and plentiful copies of manuscripts. Unlike other ancient books, thousands of partial and complete copies of Bible books exist dating within 50 to 100 years of the events described.
4. The Bible, though it was written by nearly 40 authors in three different languages and in diverse locations over a period of 1500 years, presents a unified picture of the Glory of God and His plan to rescue fallen humanity.
5. Jesus and the apostles affirm that the Bible is the Word of God.

A Bit More Detail about Christianity

The following sections derive from the Bible and add a bit of depth to what was said above about the teachings of Christianity. More information is available from my web site, www.multimediaapologetics.com.

God

There is one God, but three persons in that God: Father, Son, and Holy Spirit. Together, they are known as the Trinity and sometimes the Godhead. Each person of the Trinity is God and they are in perfect union with one another.

God is the standard of all that is good. He cannot tolerate or condone sin in any way because it is completely contrary to His perfect nature. We say that God is holy because He is free of imperfection and evil. God is all-powerful and all-knowing. He is the author of all that exists. His love, justice, and truth are perfect.

Creation

God, Jesus, and the Holy Spirit were present at the creation of the universe. They existed when the universe did not. God brought the universe into existence through Jesus. The Bible does not tell us how long ago this happened. All that was created by God was very good including man and woman. The first man and the first woman were Adam and Eve. All human beings who ever lived are descendents of Adam and Eve.

The Fall

God placed Adam and Eve in the Garden of Eden to tend His creation. There were few rules. Adam and Eve were to be fruitful and to multiply, and they were to refrain from eating from or touching the tree at the middle of the garden. God gave Adam and Eve freedom to obey or disobey Him. Adam and Eve were tempted by Satan and they disobeyed God. Something changed drastically in them and in the world around them. Sin had entered the world and corrupted God's good creation. Adam and Eve were changed forever. They were permanently corrupted by sin in what appears to be a genetic change. The result was that sinful humanity was alienated from a perfect God who is the standard of what is right and good. Since all humanity is descended from Adam and Eve, all humans inherited a sin nature. It is a fact of human experience that that sin nature shows up in different ways in different people and that there are no perfect people.

The Solution to Human Alienation from God

God in His perfect justice cannot look the other way at the sins of humans. However, in His perfect love, He has made a way for humans to be reconciled to Him. For God, the Creator of the universe, the only acceptable sacrifice and payment for the sins of the world was His Son's suffering and death on the cross. At the cross, God in human flesh paid the price for the sins of the world. All who truly repent of their sins and believe in the death and resurrection of Jesus will be granted eternal life in the presence of God in heaven.

Chapter 12
Why We Each Need Jesus

The Reality of Sin in Our Own Lives

God has made His rules for how we must live our lives plain in the Ten Commandments. Let's consider for a moment how we would stack up against God's Ten Commandments on our own merits.

Think for a moment. Have you ever told a lie, even a little white lie, perhaps a lie of convenience, or to spare someone's feelings? It is still a lie. Have you ever fudged the numbers on your income tax—a few more deductions here, a bit less income there? Have you ever exaggerated on a job application or resume? No doubt, there is not a person who has not broken the commandment not to lie in some way.

How about stealing? Have you ever taken something that did not belong to you, anything at all, perhaps just a pencil, a paper clip, or a few coins?

How about adultery? Maybe you are comforted that you have never physically cheated on your spouse, but Jesus says that if we even look on another person with lust, we have committed adultery in our heart!

How about murder? Perhaps you are safe there, but once again, not so fast. Jesus says if we are even angry with our brothers, we have committed murder in our heart.

How about taking the Lord's name in vain? Have you ever done that? Most likely you have.

What about having other gods before the Lord? Maybe we don't have idols made of stone or metal, but what about money, things, and activities? Do you ever put these before God? Can any of us really say that we put God first in our lives all of the time?

Have you ever skipped church, just gone through the motions of getting there and sitting there, or avoided church completely? If so, you have not kept the Sabbath.

How about coveting? Have you ever wanted something that belonged to your neighbor? Maybe you have been a bit jealous? We have all fallen short of God's perfect standard!

Why Good People Will Not Be in Heaven

I won't go through the rest of the commandments but I think if we are honest, we have to admit that we have all broken the Ten Commandments many times throughout our lives. The breaking of God's commandments is sin, and sin erects a barrier between us and God who is perfect. When we say we are a "good person" we are comparing ourselves to the standards of the world; but that standard is far too low! We miss the point that the true standard is perfection. That is God's standard, and when we compare ourselves to it, it should be obvious that we have all fallen short of the perfection of God. The world's standards are not God's standards. We can never be good enough to be in the presence of a perfect God on our own merits. We love to hear about the perfect love of God but are less interested in the perfect justice of God. But ignoring it will not diminish it. A perfect God must judge sin.

No, good people will not be in heaven. Only righteous people will be in heaven. Only righteous people will be in heaven before a righteous God. On our own merits we can never achieve righteousness, but thanks be to God, He credits righteousness to each of us when we repent of our sins and truly believe in his Son!

God's Nature Demands a Penalty for Sin

The prophet Habakkuk tells us that God is so pure that he cannot even look on wickedness, and that is exactly what sin is. God has not just made some arbitrary standard in order to set us up for failure. No, He has given us His law because it is His standard. Since God is the owner and creator of the universe, His standard must be satisfied.

God is the one and only standard of what is good, and what is good is what is consistent with His nature. Because God is just, He must judge sin. God cannot go against His own perfect nature.

If God is So Loving, Why Must He Punish People?

God's perfect justice demands that there be a penalty for sin. Some say, "If God is so loving there cannot be a hell." The problem with this assessment is that it overlooks that God is simultaneously perfectly loving and perfectly just. He can't give up on justice to show His love.

Consider the hypothetical situation where someone breaks into your home and brutally murders your spouse while you are away. The responsible individual is brought to trial. The evidence is clear-cut and the murderer is convicted by the jury. At sentencing, the judge allows the murderer to speak before the sentence is read. The murderer begins to cry, says he is sorry, and promises never to do it again. The judge then reads the sentence: the murderer is to be set free because he is sorry for what he has done. The judge bangs the gavel, and the murderer freely leaves the courtroom while you sit there in agony contemplating your broken life.

No civilized people would stand for such an outrage. There would be cries for the removal of the judge from the bench. This is a ridiculous outcome to this tragic story, but it represents exactly how people often think God will interact with them. They assume, as I have said, that God is so loving that He will never punish them. They assume, like the incompetent judge, that God will just overlook their sins.

The outcome is ridiculous because justice is neglected! No good human judge is going to let a law breaker go scot free—the murderer has broken God's commandments and owes a great debt to society whether he is sorry or not. Neither should we think that the Perfect Judge, God, will let us off scot free when we break His laws. An all-knowing God cannot just overlook the sins we have committed!

God's love and justice must be both satisfied in His dealings with his creatures. Each of us throughout our lives breaks God's laws in many ways. If we are honest with ourselves, if we look deep inside, we will find some very unpleasant things. Can you imagine if every evil thought you ever had and every evil deed you ever committed flashed up on a giant screen for everyone in the world to see? Can you honestly say that you would be proud of all your thoughts and deeds?

If God is perfectly good and we are corrupt fallen people by God's standards, are we hopelessly destined to be eternally separated from God? By no means—God has provided a solution to this dilemma!

Here Is Where the Love of God Comes In

God knows that His children cannot pay the debt for their sins. God descended from the heavenly realm to offer payment for the sins of His children. Jesus Christ came clothed in humanity to pay the price for our sin debt through his sacrifice on the cross.

Nothing the guilty murderer described above could do would change the fact of his guilt. Likewise, nothing we can do will change the fact that we are guilty before God. We had a sin nature at birth and we have sinned throughout our lives. It therefore by the grace of God that we are saved, because nothing we can do will remove our guilt. God reaches down to us. God, through Jesus, is the author of our salvation.

God, in His amazing love for his creatures, made a way that they could be reunited with Him. God sent Jesus on a mission to rescue fallen humanity. The sacrifice for the sins of the world that was acceptable to God was the suffering and death of Jesus Christ on the cross. Christ died for our sins. He died the death that we deserved and paid the price for our sins. His death on the cross atoned for our sins (Matt 20:28; Gal. 3:13). Through the death of His sinless Son Jesus, we are reconciled to God, and the righteousness of Jesus Christ is credited to all who believe in him. (2 Cor. 5:18-21; 1 Pet. 2:24; Heb 9:28; Isa. 53:4-6)

Through the work of Christ, the sins of those who repent and believe have been nailed to the cross, and God has dropped the charges lodged against us. In short, believers are forgiven and their sin debt is paid in full (Colossians 2:13).

Jesus Christ is God revealed in the flesh. He led a sinless life. Jesus did something for us that no human could do. He saves us from drowning in our sin because He is sinless. Jesus is able to save us from drowning in a sea of sin because He is not drowning. A drowning person cannot save another drowning person. They both will drown. By believing in Christ, we accept the sacrifice that He made on our behalf and we are reconciled to God.

Those who trust in Jesus Christ as Lord and Savior are granted salvation, not on the basis of works, but through the mercy and the grace of God. Believers in Jesus are renewed and regenerated by the Holy Spirit. God works on believers throughout their lives to prepare them for eternity in His presence. No human could hope for a more excellent destiny.

A Dark Side

There is a dark side to all of this. Eternity in God's presence is only for those who repent of their sins and truly believe in Jesus. Consider Jesus' words:

> For God so loved the world, that He gave His only begotten Son, that whoever believes in Him shall not perish, but have eternal life. For God did not send the Son into the world to judge the world, but that the world might be saved through Him. He who believes in Him is not judged; he who does not believe has been judged already, because he has not believed in the name of the only begotten Son of God. (John 3:16-18)

Those who truly believe in Jesus are sure to be with God for eternity. Those who do not believe in Jesus are sure to be separated from God for eternity.

The Eternal Destiny of All People

No person knows the eternal destiny of another person. God will decide where each of us will spend eternity. However, God has made His divine game plan quite clear.

The Bible tells us that after we live our lives, we will be judged by the perfect Judge (Heb. 9:27). There will be no reincarnation, second chance, or trap door escapes. There are only two possible places where humans will spend eternity: heaven or hell. This is what Jesus teaches. (John 3:16-18) Those who have rejected, denied, or ignored Jesus will be separated from God forever in a place called hell. I wish I could give you better news, but I can't do so and still tell you the truth of what the Bible says. Those who repent of their sins, receive Jesus in this life, and truly believe that He is the resurrected Son of God will be granted access to heaven.

There is no middle ground described in the Bible. Those who ignore Jesus or deny that He is the Son of God have rejected Him and have cast their lot with the outcasts.

Even after reading this, many will make their own salvation plan. They will fall back on, "I believe that all good people will go to heaven." When people say this, they are making themselves out to be the lord of the universe. They certainly can't prove that all good people will go to heaven.

The Lord of the universe has spoken to us through a prophetic, divine book. He has said that only those who believe in His Son will gain access to heaven. It's God's universe. He created it from nothing! It follows that God is the one who will define how His creatures can gain access to His heaven.

Heaven

Heaven is the place where God and Christ are in charge (Mt 22:44). It is a place of perfection and great beauty where there will be no sickness, pain, or death. There will be no judgment or sin. It is the place of perfect harmony where those who love God will be with God. The Father, Son, and Holy Spirit will be present there. All who die believing in Christ as their Savior will immediately be granted access to heaven. True believers of all ages will spend eternity in the presence of God, basking in His glory and singing His praises.

Hell

Hell is a troublesome topic for many, so consider the following before you reject the reality of hell. Can you imagine spending your life ignoring God, making jokes about Jesus freaks and Christians, or rejecting what the Bible teaches about proper living, and ending up in a place like heaven where the residents sing praises to God and Jesus for eternity? For the person who has ignored God or rejected God by denying His Son, heaven would not be the place he or she would want to be. In fact, to someone who ignores or rejects Jesus, heaven would

Earth To Eternity

be a place of torment, a living hell.

Jesus, the one who proved He is the Son of God by fulfilling the Messianic prophecies, mentions hell about 21 times, referring to it as hell, the outer darkness, or, the place of weeping and gnashing of teeth. Hell is a place of misery and eternal punishment and complete separation from God. It is not a good place. Hell is the place where Satan, his angels, and those who have ignored or rejected Jesus will spend eternity. The unrighteous and their father Satan, will be cast into the furnace of fire prepared for them where there will be weeping and gnashing of teeth (Mt. 13:41-42).

Think about it. If there is an eternal heaven, there must be an eternal hell to allow those who despise, reject, or ignore God to be separated from Him eternally. God allows his enemies to have their own way. God considers those who reject His Son to be enemies along with Satan and his rebellious angels.

Thirteen
Another Pass Through Important Stuff

The Bible clearly tells us that God is loving and just. He has shown His love for us by sending His Son (John 3:16). So when we reject His Son, we reject Him, because He is the one who sent His Son in the first place. If we reject Him in this earthly life, He will not force us to spend eternity with Him. God's perfect love for us does not allow Him to force us to love Him. God allows us to resist His advances. He allows His creatures to freely choose. He loves the world and He is wooing it through His Son and the Holy Spirit, but the reality is that many will spurn His love.

This life is preparation for eternity. If we hate the things of God in this life, we aren't going to like them any better in eternity. A loving God will not force those who do not love Him to spend eternity with Him. For those who ignore, deny, and despise God and His Son, God has prepared a place called hell. The good news is, that because of Jesus' work on the cross, no one needs to go to hell, but the reality is that some will.

Peter says:

> The Lord is not slow about His promise, as some count slowness, but is patient toward you, not wishing for any to perish but for all to come to repentance. (2 Peter 3:9)

God wants everyone to come to an understanding of their sinful nature in this life, and to come to the point of repenting and asking Him for forgiveness. God does not want anyone to perish, but a just God must separate those from Him who cannot even acknowledge their sinful, corrupt, human nature.

Alienation from God and the punishment that results from it can be avoided. Jesus said:

89

Earth To Eternity

For God so loved the world, that He gave His only begotten Son, that whoever believes in Him shall not perish, but have eternal life. For God did not send the Son into the world to judge the world, but that the world might be saved through Him. He who believes in Him is not judged; he who does not believe has been judged already, because he has not believed in the name of the only begotten Son of God. (John 3:16-18)

Those who repent and believe in Jesus will avoid the torment of hell. There is no better time than the present to repent and believe. Our existence on this planet is tentative at best. The next minute of our lives is not guaranteed. God calls us to receive Jesus. The question is: What will you do with Jesus?

People are skeptical about Christianity even though it is supported by compelling evidence. Instead, the world chases after the flimsiest of flimflam. Why? The world is full of fakes and delusions that consume young and old. They prevent us from seeing the obvious truth of the uniqueness of Christ in the entire history of the human race. They obscure our path and cloud our judgment and prevent us from apprehending the great unassailable, imperishable truth in the universe, a truth that comes with eternal consequences.

The truth is this: Humans fell into bondage to sin by their willful disobedience to God. The God of the universe is a God of love and justice. Because of His just nature, he must punish sin just as we would expect a good human judge to punish a crime.

Because of His love, God made a way for humanity to be redeemed. The sins of those who receive Jesus, and believe in Him are forgiven through His shed blood on the cross as a payment for the sins of the world. Because of Christ's victory on the cross, to all who receive Him, He gave the right to become children of God. But we must receive Him, and receiving Him means repenting of our sins, believing in Him, and obeying His commands. If we love Him we will obey his commands.

The world rejects God's plan of salvation because it requires humility and submission to Him. The world rejects God's plan of salvation because it requires surrendering authority to God. We must humbly go before the author of the universe. The clay will not tell the potter what to do!

90

Jesus is the Good Shepherd. He stands at the door of your heart knocking, waiting for you to open the door.

According to the Scriptures, Jesus came to divide those who reject Him from those who believe in Him. That is tough medicine to swallow. In this life, He forces us to receive Him or to reject Him. If we ignore Him, we have rejected Him. He forces us to laud Him as God in the flesh, or discard Him as inconsequential. He forces us to affirm His Deity, or to live in eternal separation from Him.

Jesus calls us to believe. We cannot slip into eternity on the wrong side of this issue, for eternity hangs in the balance. Heaven and hell hang in the balance. For heaven's sake, receive the one who can take away your sins and save you from the righteous judgment of God. When you trust in Jesus, your sin debt is cancelled. When you reject Jesus, you stand before God on your own merits and *you* will be required to pay for your sins. It is up to you. Jesus can pay for your sins through His finished work on the cross, or *you* can pay for your sins.

Jesus Christ is the way, the truth, and the life, and no one gains access to the Father except through him.

Can't Quite Go There?

Would you like to believe in Jesus but find yourself dealing with skepticism and doubt? If so, I have been in the place that you are currently at. I believe if you ask God to help you find the truth, He will do just that. Ask God to forgive your sins and ask Him to show you the truth. The Lord is patient with us. He does not want anyone to perish, but for all to come to repentance.

91

Fourteen
How the World Will Really End

Ask a group of people how they think the world will end and I suspect you will get a wide range of answers. Some will say that the world will end when a comet strikes the earth and fills the atmosphere with dust and water vapor, thus causing the earth to grow cold. Others will say that the earth will be taken over by UFO's. Some will even say that machines will become so sophisticated that they will take over the world. Some believe that we will destroy ourselves through nuclear war. Some think the truth is hidden in the prophecies of Nostradamus. Hollywood has its own opinions, but the truth of the matter is plainly revealed in a book that shows itself to be of divine origin. There is no need to speculate and postulate. The Bible clearly lays out the events leading to the end of the world.

End Times Events Are Clearly Explained

People put ridiculous unsupported theories of the end of the world on par with the Bible, but that is a big mistake. Hundreds of Bible prophecies have already been fulfilled, which leads me to the conclusion that we should take what the Bible says about the end of the world very seriously.

The end could come at any time. In my view, this fact provides all of us with great incentive to make sure that we are ready. Paul says that the day of the Lord (a common reference to the end of the world in the Bible), will come like a thief in the night (1 Thessalonians 5:2). The world will be surprised when Jesus returns. If you are alive when Jesus returns and you have not received Him, it will be too late.

I have no doubt that things will play out according to the Bible. The world is changing rapidly. Everything is falling into place in a manner consistent with the Bible's prophecies about the end times. The Bible provides us with a clear picture of the signs of the end times as we will see below.

The Main Event

One of the fundamental doctrines of Christianity is that Jesus will return according to His promise. The world scoffs at the notion of Jesus returning, but it does so at its own peril, for the one who came as a gentle lamb and good shepherd, will return as a conquering king and as mighty God. Yes, the world scoffs at the notion of Jesus' return, but those who follow Jesus, eagerly await His return because all that is wrong with the world will be instantly made right.

Both the Old and New Testaments are filled with promises of the Second Coming of Christ. There are hundreds of references to it in the Old Testament in the Psalms and writings of the prophets, and over 300 references to it in the New Testament. Among the New Testament Books, 23 of the 27 refer to this great event. For every prophecy about the First Coming of Christ, there are eight regarding Christ's Second Coming.[60]

Events Preceding the Second Coming of Jesus

The Bible foretells a number of events that will take place before the Second Coming of Jesus. Jesus told his followers to "be on the alert… for you do not know the day or the hour."[61] Since Jesus ascended into heaven, followers of Jesus have been watching world events unfold so that they would not be caught unaware at His return. As events play out in a manner consistent with prophecies made about the end time, we find more confirming evidence of the divine nature of Scripture.

Increase of Evil (2 Tim. 3:1-4; Matt. 24:12)

Paul describes the situation in the last days in great detail saying:

> …in the last days difficult times will come. For men will be lovers of self, lovers of money, boastful, arrogant, revilers, disobedient to parents, ungrateful, unholy, unloving, irreconcilable, malicious gossips, without self-control, brutal, haters of good, treacherous, reckless, conceited, lovers of

Earth To Eternity

pleasure rather than lovers of God... (2 Timothy 3:1-4)

Paul paints the picture of a coarse society where everyone is absorbed with him or herself, cruel to others, and untrustworthy. People will be focused on pleasure instead of God. We certainly see that greed is rampant in our world. God has been pushed to the sidelines in the United States. Supreme Court decisions have led to the banning of prayer and the Ten Commandments in public schools. About 50,000,000 innocent babies have been ripped from their mother's womb since Roe vs. Wade.[62] What could be more brutal than that?

During the period from 1960 to 2004, violent crime increased by over 200 percent even after correcting for population growth.[63] It certainly seems that we have experienced an increase of evil. The question becomes, is this the final increase of evil?

Wars and Disasters (Matt. 24: 6-8)

Jesus says in Matthew that as we approach the end there will be, "wars and rumors of wars." Jesus then says, "nation will rise against nation, and kingdom against kingdom." Some theologians see this as a clear description of world war. If Jesus is in fact referring to world war, the twentieth century certainly demonstrated the human race's ability for conflagration on a global scale.

Linked with war in Jesus' description of the times leading up to the end are famines and earthquakes. Wikipedia provides a list of famines over the last 1,500 years, which shows the striking frequency of famine even in this age of agricultural technology and high speed transportation.[64] One author notes the significant, steady increase of earthquakes in the last 700 years. There were 157 earthquakes in the fourteenth century. During each subsequent century, the occurrence of earthquakes has increased. In the nineteenth century, 2,119 earthquakes were recorded. Clearly, technology has greatly improved the ability to detect and monitor earthquakes but nevertheless, the increase appears to be significant.[65]

How The World Will Really End

Apostasy of the Church (2 Thess. 2:3; 1 Tim. 4:1; 2 Tim. 4:3-4)

The Bible tells us that before the Second Coming of Jesus, the church will undergo apostasy, which is the falling away from the historic teachings of Christianity. Is there any evidence that we are currently in a period of apostasy?

In the 1950's, weekly church attendance in the United States was as high as 49 percent according to Gallup Polls.[66] New research indicates that weekly church attendance has dropped to below 20 percent of the population.[67] In Europe, the situation is worse and some churches are being converted into museums or homes. Church attendance is less than 3 percent of the population in some countries.[68,69] In Czechoslovakia, more people believe in UFO's than in God.[70]

Is Christianity in a period of apostasy? I would say the answer is certainly yes, the Christian world is in apostasy. Is Christianity in the final apostasy spoken of by the Apostle Paul? I don't know, but it certainly seems that the present apostasy is great and is growing.

Many older Protestant denominations have rejected, de-emphasized, or altered biblical teachings that have been held sacred in the church for thousands of years. The result of all this is that denominations and independent churches that adhere to the Bible are growing, while denominations that have departed from the Bible are shrinking. The church continues to grow rapidly in areas where it is persecuted, such as China and Africa. Jesus did say that the gates of hell would not prevail against His church.

The rejection of the teachings of Jesus and His disciples is to be expected according Jesus and the Apostle Paul. Liberal Christian denominations are rejecting the biblical teachings of the inerrancy of Scripture, the divinity of Christ, and salvation through faith in Christ alone. They have redefined marriage and supported the termination of the unborn. While these departures make their message more pleasing to people, it is not pleasing to God. Paul warned that this would happen nearly 2,000 years ago:

> For the time will come when they will not endure sound doctrine; but wanting to have their ears tickled, they will accumulate for themselves teachers in accordance to their own desires, and will

95

Earth To Eternity

turn away their ears from the truth and will turn aside to myths. (2 Timothy 4:3-4)

Paul's words clearly fit our time for many religions are man-centered and not God-centered. Some people want to remake God in their image, but the foolishness and danger of this is obvious. The temporal being cannot define the eternal being.

We live in a time when many seek to define their own morality and religion. Apart from a divine definition of morality, every person's opinion is as good as the next. All morality becomes relative. What is right for one person may be wrong according to another. The ultimate result of this is that all morality becomes relative, since right and wrong are defined by the individual.

Restoration of Israel to the Promised Land (Ezek. 36:22-28)

As discussed in Chapter 3, the Bible is clear that the Jews will be gathered back to the land of their forefathers in Palestine. In Ezekiel 36:22-28, God promises to gather the Jews from all the lands and then to purify them. The Jews are to be gathered in unbelief, but God promises to change their hearts. God will change the nation of Israel. He promises to put a new spirit in them and to soften their hearts toward Him. Clearly, a part of this prophecy has been fulfilled for the Jews are gathering to a very secular Israel and they continue to return to their homeland from the most remote places of the earth. Watch the events in Israel closely. More is to come. God promises it.

War Against Israel (Ezek. 38:1-12)

Written by a Jew exiled to Babylon nearly 2,600 years ago, the Book of Ezekiel provides a panorama of end time events for the Jewish people. As noted above, Ezekiel prophesies the return of the Jews to Israel. Ezekiel also prophesies a great war against Israel that has yet to take place. Israel will be attacked by a coalition led by Gog of the land of Magog. Magog was identified by the first century Jewish historian, Flavius Joshephus, as the region north of the Black sea and east of the Caspian Sea which seems to equate to Russia in our time. Other members of the coalition include Persia, Ethiopia, Put, Gomer, and Beth-

96

togarmah, which correspond roughly to modern day Iran, Sudan, Libya, Ukraine and Turkey.

The attack on Israel by the coalition will fail. God will intervene and the invading armies and their nations will be destroyed.[71] Given the tension in the Mideast which is mounting in our time, it would not be too surprising if an attack on Israel of the nature described by Ezekiel came to pass. We see once again, that world events appear to be falling in line with biblical prophecy.

Rapture (1 Thess. 4:13-18)

The Apostle Paul describes an amazing event where the believers in Jesus Christ from all ages (the saints) are suddenly removed from the earth:

> For the Lord Himself will descend from heaven with a shout, with the voice of the archangel and with the trumpet of God, and the dead in Christ will rise first. Then we who are alive and remain will be caught up together with them in the clouds to meet the Lord in the air, and so we shall always be with the Lord. (1 Thessalonians 4:16-17)

In this passage, the Lord Jesus descends with a call to His people. Those who died believing in Him, and all of the living who believe in Him, will be caught up to meet Him in the air. Instantaneously, they will be clothed in immortal resurrection bodies which will never die or fall ill. The saints will thereafter always remain with Jesus. Paul describes this process in his first letter to the Corinthians:

> Now I say this, brethren, that flesh and blood cannot inherit the kingdom of God; nor does the perishable inherit the imperishable. Behold, I tell you a mystery; we will not all sleep, but we will all be changed, in a moment, in the twinkling of an eye, at the last trumpet; for the trumpet will sound, and the dead will be raised imperishable, and we will be changed. For this perishable must put on the imperishable, and this mortal must put on immortality. (1 Corinthians 15:50-53)

Some interpreters have tried to lump together the Rapture

97

with the Second Coming of Jesus, but the character of these events is vastly different.

At the Rapture, Jesus meets the church in the air. Believers of all ages will be caught up in the air to meet their Lord. There is no judgment since unbelievers remain on the earth. There are no advance signs which precede the Rapture—it just happens one day.

At the Second Coming, Jesus comes with His own as a conquering King and judges the inhabitants of the earth. It will be obvious to all, believers and unbelievers that Jesus has returned. Jesus describes the signs which precede His second Coming in Matthew, Chapter 24. Jesus' Second Coming is discussed in more detail in the next chapter, but it seems quite clear that the Rapture and the Second Coming are distinct events.

Some have suggested that the Rapture is not in the Bible. In the original Greek, Paul uses the word *harpazo* to describe it, which means to suddenly remove, or to snatch or catch away. The word "rapture" comes from the Latin word *raptus* which is the Latin translation of *harpazo*. Clearly, the concept of the Rapture is in Paul's description above.

Most theologians believe the Rapture of the church will precede the Great Tribulation. In the Book of Revelation, there are 16 mentions of the church in the first three chapters, and there is no mention of the church in Chapters 6 through 16 which describe the Great Tribulation. It appears that the church is absent during the Great Tribulation. It is also clear in the Scriptures that believers in Jesus are not appointed to wrath:

> … you turned to God from idols to serve a living and true God, and to wait for His Son from heaven, whom He raised from the dead, that is Jesus, who rescues us from the wrath to come." (1 Thessalonians 1:9-10)

Paul is speaking to the church in Thessalonica in this passage, but his message extends to all who believe in Jesus. If believers are to be rescued from the "wrath to come," then they should not expect to be on earth during the Great Tribulation which is referred to as the great day of God's wrath (Rev. 6:15-17). Blessed are those who repent and believe before the return of the Lord. It seems clear that they will be spared the wrath to come.

Emergence of the Antichrist (2 Thess. 2:1-12; Matt. 24:15-21; Daniel 7:8-24)

An evil personality at the center of end time events is the Antichrist. With respect to the revealing of the Antichrist, the man of lawlessness spoken of by Paul, speculation has been rampant since the early church. A few of the candidates named have included the Roman Emperors, Popes, Martin Luther, Napoleon, and Hitler. Clearly, many have erred in attempting to name the Antichrist and we must be careful in assigning an identity to him. His exact identity is a mystery, but the force behind him is clearly identified in Scripture. Paul tells us that the coming of the lawless one, the Antichrist, is in accord with the activity of Satan.

Some names used in the Bible to refer to the Antichrist include the beast, the man of lawlessness, the ruler who will come, the little horn, the man of sin, and the Abomination of Desolation (Jesus and the prophet Daniel use this last name).

What will the Antichrist be like? He will be a political genius who will likely arise from a nation in the region of the former Roman Empire. He will at first be lauded as a peacemaker. He will be a charismatic man possessing supreme self-confidence, and he will be capable of performing signs and wonders. He receives his authority from Satan and is opposed to all that is of God. He will seek to be worshipped by the world, but his time will be short, for ultimately he will be thrown into the lake of fire. The Antichrist will at first look very good, but the world will soon know that he is very, very bad.

One World Government and Religion (Rev. 13:1-18)

Revelation speaks of another beast, an unholy assistant to the first beast, the Antichrist. The second beast performs signs, such as calling down fire from heaven, which deceives those who live upon the earth. He causes the people of the earth to worship the first beast, the Antichrist. He causes the entire world to receive the mark of the beast on their right hand or forehead. Those who refuse will be unable to buy or sell, and as such, will

99

Earth To Eternity

be unable to participate in commerce of any sort.

The Great Tribulation (Matt. 24:15-21; Rev. 7:14; Rev. 4:1-19:21)

Jesus speaks of a time of great and unprecedented peril upon the earth saying,

> For then there will be a great tribulation, such as has not occurred since the beginning of the world until now, nor ever will. (Matthew 24:21)

Theologians conclude, based upon Daniel's prophecies, that the period of this tribulation will be seven years in duration. These years will be marked by disasters of increasing magnitude, progressing from the seal judgments, to the trumpet judgments, and finally to the bowl judgments. This series of horrific judgments is described in the Book of Revelation, Chapters 6 through 16. They commence with war and famine and conclude with devastations of large parts of the earth, signs in the heavens, and the greatest earthquake in history. It is during this period that the Antichrist will dominate the world stage.

Among God's purposes for this period are to punish those who reject His Son and blaspheme His name, and to cause those who are living during that time to decide who they will follow, Christ or the Antichrist.

You will not want to be on the earth during the Great Tribulation.

Fifteen
The Return of Jesus

Are We In the End Times?

For as long as the church has existed, followers of Jesus have pondered this question, and many believed that they were in fact living in the end times. We might be, or we might be approaching it, or perhaps it is still in the distant future. No one knows for sure. We do know however that it is coming.

There is no better time than the present to receive Jesus. Jesus could come back today or it could be hundreds of years from now. Jesus said that no one knows the day that the world will end. While it is important to watch for the signs of Jesus' return discussed above, we must refrain from setting dates. The world may continue in a period of decline for some time. Perhaps there will even be revival, and people will turn back to God. The important thing is that we are ready when Jesus returns for His church at the Rapture.

One of the great end time passages in the Bible is found in the twenty-fourth chapter of the Book of Matthew which records Jesus' words to His disciples during the Passion Week, the week Jesus was crucified. Jesus had just told His disciples that the temple in Jerusalem would be completely destroyed saying "not one stone here will be left upon another."[72] As described in Chapter 3, this prophecy was fulfilled in A.D. 70 when the Romans destroyed Jerusalem.

The disciples were apparently troubled by what Jesus had told them. A while later, when Jesus was sitting on the Mount of Olives which is adjacent to the Temple Mount, the disciples gathered around Jesus to ask Him about the signs that would precede His coming at the end of the age. Matthew records this:

101

Earth To Eternity

As He was sitting on the Mount of Olives, the disciples came to Him privately, saying, "Tell us, when will these things happen, and what will be the sign of Your coming, and of the end of the age?" And Jesus answered and said to them, "See to it that no one misleads you. For many will come in My name, saying, 'I am the Christ,' and will mislead many. You will be hearing of wars and rumors of wars. See that you are not frightened, for those things must take place, but that is not yet the end. For nation will rise against nation, and kingdom against kingdom, and in various places there will be famines and earthquakes. But all these things are merely the beginning of birth pangs. Then they will deliver you to tribulation, and will kill you, and you will be hated by all nations because of My name. At that time many will fall away and will betray one another and hate one another. Many false prophets will arise and will mislead many. Because lawlessness is increased, most people's love will grow cold. But the one who endures to the end, he will be saved. This gospel of the kingdom shall be preached in the whole world as a testimony to all the nations, and then the end will come." (Matthew 24:3-14, NASB95)

Jesus says some very important things in this passage. He says that His Second Coming will be preceded by many individuals claiming to be the Christ (Greek for Messiah) and that they, along with false prophets, will lead many astray. This, of course, has been happening through the ages.

Muhammad lived hundreds of years after Jesus, and Muslims claim him to be the final and greatest prophet whose teaching superseded that of Jesus. Many others have come along throughout the years claiming to have revelation superior to Jesus' words in the New Testament, including Joseph Smith, founder of the Mormon Church, and Charles Taze Russell, founder of the Jehovah's Witnesses. Every now and then someone comes along claiming to be the Messiah or God in the flesh. The point Jesus is making here is that many will be mislead by these false teachers and false messiahs.

War and threats of war will be commonplace in the end times. As said earlier, some interpreters of the Bible believe that "nation rising against nation" refers to world war. Famine and earthquakes will be a staple of the end times. After these things, persecution of Christians will break out, false prophets will increase, and many will be mislead.

Because of the increased number of people breaking God's laws, people will grow cold and suspicious toward one another. The age wraps up with the preaching of the gospel, the good news of Jesus' death and resurrection as payment for the sins of the world. Once the gospel has been preached to the all the nations, the end will come. How many have still not heard the gospel in our time?—perhaps not that many, given the explosion of communication technologies in our age.

How Will Jesus Return?

Jesus describes His return a bit later in Matthew 24. It will be at the end of the Tribulation. The heavens will be shaken. Jesus says:

> ...immediately after the tribulation of those days the sun will be darkened, and the moon will not give its light, and the stars will fall from the sky, and the powers of the heavens will be shaken. And then the sign of the Son of Man will appear in the sky, and then all the tribes of the earth will mourn, and they will see the Son of Man coming on the clouds of the sky with power and great glory. And He will send forth His angels with a great trumpet and they will gather together His elect from the four winds, from one end of the sky to the other. (Matthew 24:29-31)

The sign of Jesus will appear in the sky. It is unknown exactly what that sign is. Everyone on earth will be aware that Jesus has returned however.

All the nations of the earth will mourn, because they missed the boat. They denied God, and they denied His Son, and now they are confronted with the reality that the gospel message is true: Jesus really did rise from the dead. The nations mourn. They have no cause for celebration because, like many people today, they have refused to repent, and they have ignored or rejected Jesus! And like many people today, they will be separated from God for all eternity in hell. It is not necessary for anyone to spend eternity in hell. God calls all people to receive his Son, but He will not force you to receive Him. The decision is yours.

Earth To Eternity
The World After Jesus Returns (Revelation 19-20)

When Jesus returns, He will crush the rebel forces of the Antichrist, and He will reign in Jerusalem for a millennium (1,000 years) with His saints (believers of all ages). The saints of all ages were clothed in immortal bodies at the Rapture. Those who came to believe in Jesus during the Great Tribulation will enter the millennium in normal human bodies. They will have children and repopulate the world while Jesus reigns with His saints in Jerusalem. Satan will be bound during the millennium, and the world will be united in Christ.

At the end of the thousand year reign of Christ in Jerusalem, Satan will be let loose to instigate a final rebellion. Why would God allow this? Perhaps to allow humans born during the millennium to once again freely choose between Him and Satan. God does not want automatons, but rather those who have freely chosen Him under the influence of the Holy Spirit. This final rebellion will be quelled. Satan and all who followed him will be cast into the Lake of Fire for eternity.

A New Heaven and a New Earth will be constituted, which will last for all eternity, for the old heavens and the old earth will pass away.

God's message throughout the ages has not changed. We are challenged in the same way as Joshua challenged the Israelites:

> If it is disagreeable in your sight to serve the Lord, choose for yourselves today whom you will serve: whether the gods which your fathers served which were beyond the River...but as for me and my house, we will serve the Lord. (Joshua 24:15)

Through our actions we choose whether we will follow gods of our own making or the God who spoke the universe into existence, who has communicated plainly to His people through the Bible. Whom will you choose? Whom will you serve? Where will you spend eternity? Only you can answer these questions.

Sixteen
Epilogue

As Christians, we are called to speak the truth in love. Even though I may not know you, as a fellow human being, I want all people to find the truth that I am convinced of beyond the shadow of a doubt. If Christianity is true, as I believe the evidence clearly demonstrates, the most loving thing Christians can do is share it with others so that they can come to believe in Jesus and spend eternity in heaven.

My purpose here is not to scare people, but the consequences of not heeding Jesus' message are dire. We are all on a journey in this life. The purpose of this life is to seek God and to find Him in the person of Jesus Christ. That is what the Bible tells us. Don't let this leg of your journey end in failure. There will not be a second chance. The journey is not about acquiring possessions and power as the world tells us. It is about something much more important—finding the truth.

Given all that has been said in the previous chapters, I often wonder why so many fail to take the claims of Christianity seriously, and why so many reject God by denying Him and being skeptical about Him and the mission of Jesus Christ. I wonder why are there so many atheists and agnostics in the world, when God's plan to rescue humanity was so clearly prophesied hundreds of years before Jesus was born?

Blaise Pascal lived in the 17th century when the enlightenment was in full swing along with skepticism about the claims of Christianity. Pascal was a great French scientist and philosopher, surrounded by atheists, skeptics, and agnostics. He was also a devout Christian. Pascal sought for a way to convey to his friends and acquaintances the danger of their skepticism. He formulated a logical argument because he lived in the Age of

Earth To Eternity

Reason, a time when philosophers and scientists had found that truth could be determined by the application of logic and reason. Pascal's logical argument came to be called Pascal's Wager.

The essence of Pascal's Wager is this: If one chooses to believe in God, that individual has nothing to lose but everything to gain. If you choose to believe that Christianity is true, and you turn out to be wrong, what do you lose? You lose nothing, but rather gain a life filled with purpose, meaning, and moral structure, all of which lead to good. However, if you choose to reject Christianity, and Jesus as your Savior, and you are wrong, you will lose everything for eternity.

Faced with these choices, Pascal reasoned with his atheist and agnostic friends that the only logical choice in this life was to choose to believe that Christianity is true, and that Jesus really is the Savior of the world.

When we think carefully through Pascal's Wager, it would seem that we must agree with him. In fact, it seems that the whole world should see the wisdom of Pascal's Wager because atheism and agnosticism are really bad bets. What can be possibly gained by denying the obvious existence of God?—perhaps the pursuit of illicit and worldly pleasures with a clear conscience? But does that really make being an atheist or pagan worthwhile, when one has to risk eternal torment for the fleeting pleasures of the flesh?

It is never too late to repent and believe in Jesus. In sincerely doing so, you assure your place in heaven for eternity.

May God bless your investigation and your journey. May you call upon His name and ask Him to reveal the truth to you.

Appendix
Answers to Tough Questions

Isn't truth really relative?

The statement "truth is relative" is a self-defeating statement. If truth is relative, the statement "truth is relative" is also relative, which means that it is not true for all times, places, and peoples. If it is not true for all times, places, and peoples, you should not be concerned about it because it may not apply to you.

The reality is that all truth is absolute. Truth is what corresponds to reality. My understanding of the truth may be wrong, but that does not change the truth. Men first walked on the moon on July 21, 1969. This is a truth that is absolute, meaning that it is true for all times, places, and peoples. If I sincerely believe that the first moonwalk occurred in 1983, that does not change the fact that it actually happened on July 21, 1969. Even if someone in China is not aware of the moon walk, it is still true for them that the first moonwalk occurred on July 21, 1969. In fact, it is true for all people who will ever live. One's knowledge or understanding of the truth does not change the actual truth. Whether one accepts or rejects the moonwalk does not change the fact that the moonwalk is a fact of history and that it occurred on a certain date. Humans are not in a position to know all truth, but God is, and one day, it will be revealed.

The Bible claims that Jesus is the only way to God. If this statement is true, as I believe it is based upon the evidence presented in this book, then it is true for all people.

Am I really here?

Some have suggested that life is merely an illusion. It

should be fairly easy to test this. If one were to thrust one's hand into a pot of boiling water, one would certainly feel pain. This is easy to test for anyone who doubts it. Clearly, illusions do not feel pain. Therefore, we conclude that our existence is tangible and physical.

What about the lost books of the New Testament?

While it is true that were many gospels around, they were rejected by the early church because they were not written by authors close to the events when they actually occurred. The gospel writers Matthew and John were Apostles who followed Jesus throughout His earthly ministry. Mark was a close associate of the Apostle Peter. Luke was a traveling companion and co-worker of the Apostle Paul. The New Testament gospel writers wrote their gospels within a few decades of Jesus' crucifixion.

The books left out of the New Testament were written 100 to 200 years or more after the crucifixion by individuals who were not eyewitnesses. They include the Gospel of Phillip, the Gospel of Mary and the Gospel of Thomas. They were discovered in Egypt several hundred miles from Jerusalem, and are filled with Gnostic teachings. The Gnostics were a cult with a hodgepodge of varying beliefs borrowed from the Jews, Greeks, various philosophers, and Christianity. The Gnostics merged many religious beliefs of the day so they were not Christians.[73]

The Gnostics' beliefs and claims were rejected by the early church because they didn't agree with the Apostles' eyewitness testimony. It is important to remember that the lost books of the Bible weren't really lost. It is much more accurate to say that they were rejected by the early church because they lacked credibility.

What about those who have not heard about Jesus, will they be condemned to hell?

First, there is no avoiding it, the Bible clearly teaches that Jesus is the only way to heaven (John 3:16-18; 1John 5:12, Acts 4:12).

Second, it should be considered that the One who created the universe owns all that is in it. Nothing that is in the universe

108

would exist unless God created it. We as temporal creatures have no idea what is involved in creating a universe, and so we really have no basis for criticizing how God operates His universe.

Third, the Bible tells us that people from every nation of the earth will be in heaven, so clearly people from every nation will have heard about Jesus (Rev. 7:9).

Fourth, the Apostle Paul tells us in the Book of Acts that God determined exactly when and where each person would live so that people would seek Him and perhaps find Him (Acts 17:26-28). The God of the Bible is all-knowing and all-powerful, and thus He is able to place each person that will respond to Him exactly where they should be on the earth, at exactly the right time so that they will hear about Jesus. A perfect example of God providing for those who reach out to Him is found in the story of the centurion Cornelius recounted in Acts 10.

All will agree in the end that God, in His perfect justice, has been completely fair and judged each person perfectly.

What does it mean to repent?

In the first chapter of Mark, Jesus tells all who will listen to repent and believe. The word repent in this passage comes from the Greek *metanoéō* which means to change the mind, to relent. Theologically, it involves regret or sorrow, accompanied by a true change of heart toward God. Billy Graham once said that true repentance is being sorry enough to stop sinning. It is never too late to call out to God and to repent and believe. Now is the appointed time to seek God.

How do I become a Christian?

Christians are followers of Jesus Christ. The Apostles' formula was simply stated in Acts 2 in Peter's address to a large assembly of Jews. Peter made it clear to them that they had crucified the Messiah and they were greatly distressed. The Jews asked Peter what they should do. Peter replied:

> Repent, and each of you be baptized in the name of Jesus Christ for the forgiveness of your sins; and you will receive the gift of the Holy Spirit. (Acts 2:38)

Earth To Eternity

We must recognize that we are sinners and repent of our sins just as the Jews did that day. In seeking baptism in the name of Jesus Christ, we are publicly affirming that we believe in Him, trust in Him, and desire to receive Him. We must do this in true sincerity, for God knows every person's heart. If we do all of this to please others or to put on a show, God will know.

If you are not ready to take these steps, I encourage you to call out to God and ask Him to reveal the truth to you and to help you believe. Turn to His Scriptures, praying to God as you read. The Gospel of John is an excellent place to start.

The Christian life is just that, it is not a Christian moment. It is meant to be lived in fellowship with other Christians until your days on this earth are completed. Seek out mature Christians who can help you on your journey. Good churches publicly and regularly uphold the Bible as the inspired, inerrant Word of God. If you do not hear these words in the church you are attending, you need to find another church. It may be a storefront or it may be a large stone building. That doesn't matter. What matters is that the people in that church seek to live their lives according to what the Bible teaches and are desirous of worshipping, praising, and serving God with their entire being.

Why doesn't God just let everyone into heaven?

If you really love someone, will you force them to do something against their will? It is precisely because God is loving that He has given us free will. God will not force us to love Him. God will not force people who have rejected Him or denied His existence to be in His presence for eternity. One of critical aspects of Christian life is sanctification; that is, patterning one's life after the example of Christ. Through this lifelong quest to become more Christ-like under the influence of the Holy Spirit, Christians are preparing for eternal life in the presence of God.

Jesus died for the sins of the whole world but many will not receive Christ as their Savior and believe that He is the Son of God. Eternal life is a free gift to all who receive Christ.

Would it really be fair if everyone automatically went to heaven? That would mean that those who lived a fairly moral life would be there right alongside unrepentant murderers, rapists and tyrants.

God is perfectly just. All have sinned and fallen short of the perfection of God. We owe a debt that we cannot pay. God accepts the sacrifice of His Son as payment for the sin debt of mankind, but if we deny Jesus as our Savior who will save us?

As was said earlier, we are drowning in our sin. A drowning person cannot save him or herself. God forgives the sins of those who believe in Jesus. He marks "cancelled" on the debt notice of those who have received Jesus.

Doesn't the age of the earth disprove Genesis?

Contrary to popular belief, the Bible does not tell us how old the earth is. Some Christians believe the earth is about 6,000 years old, but many do not, including many leading evangelical (Bible believing) theologians of this age and past ages.

The concept that the earth is only 6,000 years old comes from the chronology drawn up by the Irish Bishop, James Ussher, published in 1650 under the title *Annals of the Old Testament*. By adding up the ages of people in the genealogies noted in the Old Testament, and allowing six 24 hour periods for creation, Bishop Ussher concluded that God commenced the creation on the nightfall preceding October 23rd, 4,004 B.C. Ussher's chronology was printed in many versions of the King James Bible.

In the last 100 years, scientists have ridiculed creationists claiming that all Christians believe that the dinosaurs roamed the earth only a few thousand years ago when the reality is that a large number of the most prominent Bible believing theologians hold the "old earth view" that affirms the earth is very old. For clarity, the view that the earth is about 6,000 years old is referred to as the "young earth" view.

Theologians who hold the old earth view typically do so because they find gaps in the chronologies presented in the Bible; they believe that it is not as simple as adding up the ages of people in the genealogies. They have considered the events of each day of creation given in Genesis, and believe that these events required more than 24-hour periods.

One's view of the age of the earth is not a litmus test for whether or not an individual is a Christian. It is considered by

111

most to be a secondary issue and should not be allowed divide believers in Jesus. Christians on both side of this issue believe all of the important teachings of the Bible, including the inerrancy of the Bible—they just interpret the creation passages differently.

What is the Gospel?
The gospel is the good news that eternal life is available to all who repent and believe in the resurrection of Jesus and His saving work on the cross. Paul states it simply:

> Now I make known to you, brethren, the gospel which I preached to you, which also you received, in which also you stand, by which also you are saved, if you hold fast the word which I preached to you, unless you believed in vain. For I delivered to you as of first importance what I also received, that Christ died for our sins according to the Scriptures, and that He was buried, and that He was raised on the third day according to the Scriptures... (1Corinthians 15:1-4)

Why do I need Jesus?
Jesus, the God-man, is the bridge between God and man. Jesus was with God at the foundation of the universe. He was not created but existed in eternity with God before the foundation of the world. Jesus Christ is the sinless Son of God and therefore is worthy and able to save sinful humanity. If you ignore or reject Jesus, you will have to stand before God on your own merits. According to Scripture, no one is righteous, let alone perfect, so your merits will not be sufficient.

If God is perfect, why is His creation such a mess?
God's creation was good. Satan, a free creature created by God, disobeyed God and was cast out of heaven to earth. God gave Adam and Eve freedom to choose. Adam and Eve were tempted by Satan and disobeyed God. The result was that all of creation was corrupted because sin entered the world.

Humanity continues to sin because many have turned from God and none are righteous. Humanity has made God's creation a mess, but it was not originally that way. The mess is man's doing, not God's.

Why do Christians have to be so exclusive? Aren't there many ways to God?

First, Christianity does affirm that Jesus is the only way humans can gain access to heaven. This was discussed in depth earlier.

As shown in Chapter 9, all religions and belief systems are exclusive. One excludes the possibility that there is a God, one excludes all others religions except Islam, all except one exclude the possibility that Jesus is the Savior of the world. Some exclude the possibility of attaining heaven without reincarnation. All religions are exclusive if they have any beliefs they hold to be uniquely true. All religions make truth claims that in the end contradict the beliefs of other religions. Christianity is no more exclusive than any other religion. The more you become familiar with the beliefs of the various world religions, the more it will be obvious to you that all religions are exclusive. The previous chapters have presented considerable evidence that Christianity is true beyond the shadow of a doubt. The same could not be said about any other world religion.

Besides the Apostles, did the leaders of the early church really think that Jesus is God? Wasn't Jesus just promoted to "God" at the Council of Nicea in A.D. 325?

The writings of the early church fathers, the church leaders who lived just after the apostles in the first few centuries, provide a powerful witness to their belief that Jesus was the divine Son of God. In their own words, the early fathers who were the leaders, bishops, and great minds of Christianity following the Apostles, declared that Jesus is God in human flesh. Their words echo to this day and clearly contradict the notion that the doctrine of the divinity of Christ was an invention of the Council of Nicea in A.D. 325. The divinity of Christ was reaffirmed in the teachings of the early church fathers in the first century, long before the Council of Nicea, as is shown in the table on the following page.

The Divinity of Christ in the Words of the Early Church Fathers[74]		
Church Father	Date (A.D.)	Views Expressed
Clement of Rome	c. 96	*"Let us reverence Lord Jesus Christ, whose blood was given for us"*
Ignatius	c. 105	*"Continue in intimate union with Jesus Christ our God."*
Aristides	c. 125	*"The Christians trace the beginning of their religion to Jesus the Messiah. He is called the Son of the Most High God. It is said that God came down from heaven. He assumed flesh and clothed Himself with it from a Hebrew virgin. And the Son of God lived in the daughter of man."*
Justin Martyr	c. 160	*"The Father of the universe has a son. And He, being the First Begotten Word of God, is even God."*
Athenogoras	c. 175	*"There is one God and the Logos proceeding from Him, the Son. We understand the Son to be inseparable from Him."*
Irenaeus	c. 180	*"He is God, for the name Emmanuel indicates this."*
Clement of Alexandria	c. 195	*"Our Instructor is the holy God Jesus, the Word."*
Tertullian	c. 197	*"To all He is equal, to all King, to all Judge, to all God and Lord."*
Origen	c. 225	*"Jesus Christ Himself is the Lord and Creator of the soul."*
Seventh Council of Carthage	c. 256	*"Jesus Christ, our Lord and God, is the Son of God the Father and Creator."*

Christian belief in the divinity of Jesus clearly dates to the first century and was consistently reaffirmed thereafter.

114

NOTES

1. Hugh Ross, *Creator of the Cosmos* (Colorado Springs: Navpress, 2001), pp. 23-44.
2. Norman Geisler, "Causality, Principle of," *Baker Encyclopedia of Christian Apologetics* (Grand Rapids: Baker Books, 1999).
3. Stephen Meyer, *Signature in the Cell* (New York: Harper Collins, 2009), pp. 341-344.
4. Human Genome Project Information, "Frequently Asked Questions," Available Online at www.genomics.energy.gov (accessed 6/21/10).
5. Stephen Hawking, *A Brief History of Time* (New York: Bantam Books, 1988), p. 10.
6. Meyer, p. 227.
7. Lee Strobel, *The Case for a Creator* (Grand Rapids: Zondervan, 2004), pp. 229-230.
8. Jonathan Wells, Icons of Evolution (Washington, DC: Regnery, 2002), pp. 29-45.
9. Ibid.
10. Ibid.
11. Charles Darwin, *Origin of the Species*, Chapter 6, Available online at www.darwin-online.org.uk (Accessed 11/10/10).
12. Stephen Jay Gould, *The Panda's Thumb* (New York: Norton, 1982), p. 181.
13. Ibid., p. 182.
14. Richard Dawkins, *The Blind Watchmaker* (New York: Norton, 1996), p. 230.
15. Norman Geisler and William Nix, *A General Introduction to the Bible* (Chicago : Moody Press, 1996), p. 196.
16. Isaiah 49:5-6.
17. Matthew 16:16.
18. Deuteronomy 18:18-22.
19. Norman Geisler and Ronald Brooks, *When Skeptics Ask* (Grand Rapids: Baker Books, 1990), p. 115.
20. Geoffrey Bromiley, "Israel, History of the People of," *International Standard Bible Encyclopedia* (Grand Rapids: Eerdmans, 1982), Vol. 2, pp. 908-924.
21. 2 Kings 25:1-21.
22. Charles Ryrie, *Ryrie Study Bible*, (Chicago: Moody Press, 1995), p. 1302.

23. John Walvoord and Roy Zuck, eds., *The Bible Knowledge Commentary* (Colorado Springs: Victor, 1983), 2Kings 23.
24. Randall Price, *The Stones Cry Out* (Eugene: Harvest House, 1997), pp. 252-252.
25. Harold W. Hoehner, *Chronological Aspects of the Life of Christ* (Grand Rapids: Zondervan Publishing, 1977), pp. 126-39.
26. Walvoord, Daniel 9 & Nehemiah 2.
27. Peter Stoner, *Science Speaks*, Chapter 3, Available online at: www.sciencespeaks.dstoner.net (Accessed 11/11/10).
28. William Albright quoted in *Baker Encyclopedia of Christian Apologetics*, "Dead Sea Scrolls."
29. Bromiley, "Dead Sea Scrolls," Vol. 1, p. 883.
30. Geisler, *Baker Encyclopedia of Christian Apologetics*, "Dead Sea Scrolls."
31. Geisler, *A General Introduction to the Bible*, pp.196-197.
32. Gary Habermas and Michael Liacona, *The Case for the Resurrection of Jesus*(Grand Rapids: Kregel, 2004), pp. 36-40.
33. William F. Albright, *Recent Discoveries in Bible Lands* (New York: Funk and Wagnalls, 1955), p. 136.
34. Geisler, *Baker Encyclopedia of Christian Apologetics*, "New Testament Manuscripts."
35. Gleason Archer, *A Survey Of Old Testament Introduction* (Chicago: Moody Press, 1994), p. 27.
36. Archer, pp. 26-27.
37. Frederic Kenyon quoted in *Baker Encyclopedia of Christian Apologetics*, "New Testament Manuscripts."
38. Geisler, Baker Encyclopedia of Christian Apologetics, "Archaeology, New Testament."
39. William Ramsay, *St. Paul the Traveler and Roman Citizen*, Chapter 1, Available online at www.ccel.org/ccel/ramsay/ paul_roman.iv.html (Accessed 11/15/2010).
40. William Ramsay, *The Bearing of Recent Discovery on the Trustworthiness of the New Testament*, p. 222, Available online at www.archive.org/stream/bearingofrecentd00ramsuoft#page/ n7/mode/2up (Accessed 11/15/2010).
41. A. N. Sherwin-White, *Roman Society and Roman Law in the New Testament* (Grand Rapids: Baker Books, 1978), p. 189.
42. Randall Price, *The Stones Cry Out* (Eugene: Harvest House, 1997), pp. 295-318.
43. Nelson Glueck, *Rivers in the Desert* (New York: Farrar, Strauss and Cudahy, 1959), p. 31.

44. Simon Greenleaf, *Testimony of the Evangelists*, Available online at www.provisionftv.com/Articles/Testimony%20of%20the%20Evangelists.pdf (Accessed 11/15/2010).
45. Stoner, Chapter 3, (Accessed 11/15/2010).
46. John 11:25.
47. Habermas and Liacona, pp. 48-77.
48. Hippolytus, *On the Twelve Apostles*, Ante-Nicene Father, vol 5 (Accessed in the The Master Christian Library, ver. 6).
49. 1 Corinthians 15.
50. Habermas and Liacona, pp. 69-77.
51. Ryrie, Map 14.
52. Tacitus, *Annals*, Book 15:44, Available online at www.sacred-texts.com/cla/tac/a15040.htm (Accessed 7/15/10).
53. James Charlesworth, *Jesus Within Judaism* (New York: Doubleday, 1988), p. 95.
54. Julius Africanus, *On the Circumstances Connected with our Savior's Passion and His Life-giving Resurrection*, Ante-Nicene Father, vol. 6 (Accessed in the *The Master Christian Library*, ver. 6).
55. Pliny and Trajan Correspondence, Available online at the Ancient History Sourcebook, http://www.fordham.edu/halsall/ancient/pliny-trajan1.html (Accessed 7/15/10).
56. Ibid.
57. Ibid.
58. Lucian, *The Death of Peregrine*, Available online at Sacred Texts, www.sacred-texts.com/cla/luc/wl4/wl420.htm (Accessed 11/15/10).
59. I. Epstein, transl., *The Babylonian Talmud*, (London: Soncino, 1935). Vol. III, Sanhedrin 43a, p. 281.
60. Tim LaHaye and Ed Hindson, eds., "Second Coming of Christ," *The Encyclopedia of Bible Prophecy* (Eugene: Harvest House, 2004).
61. Matthew 25:13.
62. Abortion Statistics since 1973, Available online at http://www.nrlc.org/abortion/facts/abortionstats.html (Accessed 11/15/10).
63. United States Crime Rates 1960-2009, Available online at www.disastercenter.com/crime/uscrime.htm (Accessed 11/15/10).

117

64. List of Famines, Available online at http://en.wikipedia.org/wiki/List_of_famines (Accessed 11/15/10).
65. Arnold Fruchtenbaum, *The Footsteps of the Messiah* (San Antonio: Ariel Ministries, 2009), pp. 96-97.
66. Church Attendance Statistics, Available online at www.christianitytoday.com/yc/2001/003/15.88.html (Accessed 11/15/10).
67. John Marcum, "Measuring Church Attendance," Available online at www.jstor.org/pss/3512431 accessed online at http://www.jstor.org/pss/3512431 (Accessed 11/15/10).
68. Robert Manchin, "Trust Not Filling the Pews," Available online at www.gallup.com/poll/13117/religion-europe-trust-filling-pews.aspx (Accessed 11/16/10).
69. Eunice Or, "Trust in Religious Institutions does not Convey to Church Attendance," Available online at www.christiantoday.com/article/trust.in.religious.institutions.does.not.convey.to.church.attendance/ 1462.htm (Accessed 11/17/10).
70. James Gannon, "Is God Dead in Europe?," Available online at http://www.usatoday.com/news/opinion/editorials/2006-01-08-faith-edit_x.htm (Accessed 11/17/10).
71. Ryrie, Notes for Ez. 38.
72. Matthew 24:2.
73. Bromiley, "Gnosticism," Vol. 2, p 484.
74. David Bercot, ed., A Dictionary of Early Christian Beliefs (Peabody: Hendriksen, 1999), pp. 93-106.

For additional copies and bulk purchases, contact the author at:

dc.earthtoeternity@gmail.com

For additional copies and bulk purchases, contact the author at:

dc.earthtoeternity@gmail.com